The Art of Cartooning with Flash

The Art of Cartooning with Flash™

JOHN KURAMOTO, GARY LEIB, DANIEL GRAY

SYBEX® SAN FRANCISCO • LONDON

Associate Publisher: Dan Brodnitz
Acquisitions and Developmental Editor: Mariann Barsolo
Editor: Susan Hobbs
Production Editor: Dennis Fitzgerald
Technical Editor: Denise Tyler
Book Designer: Thomas Ingalls
Book Production: Owen Wolfson
Proofreaders: Jennifer Campbell, Dave Nash, Laurie O'Connell, Yariv
Rabinovitch
Indexer: Nancy Guenther
CD Coordinator: Christine Detlefs
CD Technician: Kevin Ly
Cover Designer: Lori Barra, TonBo Designs

Library of Congress Card Number: 2001096973
ISBN: 0-7821-2913-7

Manufactured in the United States of America

10 9 8 7 6 5 4 3 2 1

ACKNOWLEDGMENTS

Animation is collaboration. Even if one person made it, it's still a collaboration between that person and the audience.

I can't do a single thing without the artists I work with. Because I can't draw my way out of a paper bag, I rely on them completely to make the chunks I need to make cartoons. So to all the artists I've worked with, but especially Doug Allen, my most frequent collaborator—the man who willingly allows us to chain him to the drawing board until he finishes churning out the art—I give my heartiest thanks.

I also proffer my thanks to those who threw in their two bits and made sure my unsubstantiated claims weren't completely unfounded: Daniel Clowes, Kim Deitch, and Mark Newgarden.

—John Kuramoto

Most of all, I'd like to thank John and Gary. This is their book. I'm only a humble servant, at the service of their idea. I'm honored to have helped bring this book to print (more as an editor than as author).

This book could not have happed without the support of the good folks at Sybex, most specifically the ever-marvelous Mariann Barsolo. We were blessed to have a great team. Kudos go to: Suz Hobbs for her expert copy edits, Denise Tyler for her fine technical edits, Dennis Fitzgerald for keeping the whole thing moving, and Thom Ingalls and Owen Wolfson for a great looking book.

When we first stirred up the idea of a book on cartooning with Flash back in the summer of 2000, it was a different world. The events of September 11, 2001 have forever changed the way we live. How, I thought, could we ever laugh again?

Looking back over the history of cartooning, however, the stories and characters have gotten us through some very tough times. Your cartoons can help to continue that tradition.

—Daniel Gray

For Bonnie, of course.

—John Kuramoto

*This mighty tome is dedicated to my daughter Lila
and wife Judy, who love a good laugh as much as
I do, and with thanks to the entire staff at Twinkle
for their hard work and intense study of silliness.*

—Gary Leib

*To Deb, Ali, and Colt—my very own cast of cartoon
characters—may we never forget how to be kids.*

—Daniel Gray

CONTENTS

CHAPTER 3

Animation Basics in Flash

CHAPTER 4

CHAPTER 7

Introduction

When I first told people that I was going to write a book about character animation in Flash, the response was often, "aren't you worried about giving away all your secrets?" I suppose the belief was that making a cartoon in Flash involves a series of tricks, and if someone just knew the tricks, they too could make a cartoon. Unfortunately, it's true.

Anyone can learn Flash and start pooping out cartoons. For a while, it seemed like everyone did. But simply making something that resembles animation does not mean it will be entertaining, interesting, or the least bit amusing.

Animation is kind of like dancing. Some people are just naturals at it. Some people are kind of embarrassed to do it, but if they worked at it, they could be pretty darn good. And some people are just hopeless. The fact is, not everyone can dance. But everyone can practice and give it the old college try. All we ask is that you do it with style.

So are we giving away all our secrets? Absolutely. Are we worried?

Not in the least.

This book is full of techniques for character animation. But that's all they are: techniques. No amount of technique can make a bad story good, or an unfunny joke funny. But technique can mean the difference between halfway-decent and fantastic animation. Given the choice, I'll take fantastic. If we can help you get there, then writing this book wasn't a total waste of time.

There's any number of ways to make a Flash cartoon. This book is about the way we make cartoons at Twinkle. Make your cartoon any way you like. As long as it makes people laugh, who cares how it got on the screen? The bulk of the techniques we show you are based on character animation principles that have been around for a long time. Learn the principles, take what you can from this book, and apply it to your own methods.

If you've never used Flash before, you'll have to pick up some other book to get you up to speed. There are more books about Flash than you can shake a stick at, not the least of which is the manual that came with the program. Those books will tell you what the functions are and what the tools do. This book will tell you what to do with them, if what you want to do is make cartoons.

When I decided to get married, I also decided that I would learn to tie a bow tie. A clip on was unacceptable. So I got one, stood in front of the mirror with the instructions, and tried to figure it out. Step 1: Put it around your neck. Step 2: Cross this side over that side. Step 3: Bring this side up and over. Step 4: Put this bit over here. Okay, got it so far. Step 5: Admire your perfectly tied bow tie. What? Somehow I was supposed to go from the jumbled mass in step 4 to the perfectly tied bow tie in step 5. Eventually I figured it out through trial and error, and scrutinizing correctly tied bow ties.

I couldn't possibly tell you how to tie a bow tie, but I can tell you a little something about making cartoons in Flash. Here's to the step between 4 and 5.

—John Kuramoto

WHO SHOULD READ THIS BOOK

Uhhhh ... you should!

You might think it's pretty simple ... don't read this book unless you want to learn how to make great cartoons with Macromedia Flash. But there's more to it than that. The principles and techniques discussed in this book are, in many cases, transferable to other vector-based animation programs. So whether you're using a vector animation tool from Macromedia, Adobe, Corel, Toon Boom, or Thursday's Software Developer of Choice, you'll be able to extract a great amount of value from this book.

WHAT'S COVERED IN THIS BOOK

We're going to take you from concept through completion of a Flash cartoon. You'll learn the fundamentals and fine tweaks. While this book was written about Macromedia Flash 5, the concepts and techniques apply to version 4 and will likely apply to the next version, as well. Here's a quick chapter-by-chapter rundown of what's covered.

Chapter 1

The Twinkle method of Flash cartooning applies classic principles to the Flash environment. Chapter 1 explains the 12 classic principles of animation: squash and stretch, anticipation, staging, straight-ahead and pose-to-pose, follow-through and overlapping action, slow-in and slow-out, arcs, secondary action, timing, exaggeration, solid drawing, and appeal.

Chapter 2

In Chapter 2, Gary reveals how drawing is, at its heart, a funny business. You'll learn a bit about how to share the responsibilities within a studio while maintaining both a sense of whimsy and history.

Chapter 3

First you learned theory; now you'll begin to put it into practice. In this chapter you'll take the limitations of vector-based animation and make them a style as you discover the basics of digital puppetry.

Chapter 4

Chapter 4 goes further to demonstrate how to apply the classic principles of cartooning to Flash. You'll work with easing, arcs, squash and stretch, center points, skewing, timing, straight-ahead and pose-to-pose, exaggeration, anticipation, overshoot, follow-through and overlapping action, and secondary action.

Chapter 5

There's nothing finer than knees, elbows, and walk cycles. Chapter 5 takes the digital puppet apart as it examines the relationship between the different limbs. Walk cycles, shape tweens, looping, and facial animation are also covered.

Chapter 6

Chapter 6 covers the workflow of a Flash cartoon as you create the story and characters, build the storyboard, create, and edit the animatic with scratch dialogue, record dialogue, and (finally!) create the animation.

Chapter 7

Scene building is an integral part of the animation process. Chapter 7 details the mechanics of layout within Flash while covering the topics of backgrounds, camera moves, and transitions. You'll learn how to build a scene, loop a background, add characters and foreground elements, and combine scenes with fancy transitions.

Chapter 8

Chapter 8 is a quick jaunt into the topic of sound. The chapter provides information on streaming sound, recording, dialogue, music, sound effects, and mixing.

Chapter 9

Want to know how a masterpiece was made? Chapter 9 delivers the skinny on the making of the first episode of *Jickett's Speed Shop.* You'll learn how the episode was written and storyboarded, as well as the processes of creating the animatic and dialog recording. The meat of the chapter is a fully illustrated scene-by-scene analysis of the cartoon. The chapter is accompanied by a special version of the movie on the CD, featuring DVD-like controls so you can view the action, frame-by-frame.

Appendices

Take a drive through Appendix A before you load your Flash cartoon on your web server. The appendix provides information on file clean up, preloading, and dumping Flash out to video. Appendix B provides a resource list of books, websites, and movies. Appendix C aims to help you build better buttons with Flash.

Hardware and Software Considerations

You'll need to have Macromedia Flash installed on your computer to get the most out of this book. Flash 5 requires a minimum of 50 MB of disk space, although Macromedia recommends 70 MB or more. An 800 x 600 display and 32 MB of RAM are required. On a Macintosh, you'll need to be running System 8.1 or later on a PowerPC processor. On Windows, you'll need to be running Windows 95, 98, 2000, or NT 4 (Service Pack 3) on a 133 or better Pentium class processor. You're not likely to be happy with the minimums, however. Here are some basic tips about building a computer for Flash work:

- Get a fast processor, but don't feel that you have to buy the fastest one out there. The fastest processors do not deliver bang for the buck. Get a slightly slower processor for the best combination of price and performance.
- Stuff your computer full of RAM. A computer with lots of memory is a happy computer. And even better, RAM is cheap these days.
- Consider a dual-monitor setup. Stuff your palettes on one monitor and your Stage on the other. Some higher-end laptops can work right out of the box with dual monitors.

CD Materials

You'll find periodic reference to files on the CD for you to complete some of the exercises in the book. You'll probably want to copy these files onto your computer's hard drive to use them. The exercise files frequently include an "exercise" scene where you can start from scratch (with supplied tidbits) as well as additional scenes (as denoted by the figures) that show the progression of each exercise.

UPDATES

Stuff changes. Nowhere is this more apparent than in the geekbook world. To obtain the latest updates to this book, be sure to check the authors' websites at twinkleland.com and geekbooks.com.

ABOUT THE PERPETRATORS

Located in downtown Manhattan, Twinkle provides multi-format animation, design, and special effects for broadcast design, advertising, television animation, film, and the Internet. Gary Leib founded Twinkle in 1993. Working with famed artists Peter Bagge, Doug Allen, Daniel Clowes, Chris Ware, and Charles Burns, Twinkle has grown into a full-scale animation studio.

Gary Leib is a pop culture renaissance man whose unique creative talents and sociological insights have enlivened an impressive array of mediums, both old and new. His work as an animator, cartoonist, musician, and teacher at The School of Visual Arts in its computer animation department has won universal praise. His illustrations and cartoons have appeared in *The New Yorker*, *Musician Magazine*, *The New York Observer*, *Raw*, *Blab*, and as weekly features in *The New York Press* since 1992. In addition, Gary is also an accomplished musician, and was a founding member of the Grammy-nominated band, Rubber Rodeo. He has created original music for independent and feature films, including the critically acclaimed *Ironweed*. Gary is a graduate of the Rhode Island School of Design.

John Kuramoto is a Flash god. Before devoting his life to animation, Kuramoto was a pre-press consultant and color separator for Adrian Tomine and Daniel Clowes. For three years, John wrote the series *Imaginary Magnitude* for the monthly manga *Afternoon*, published in Japan by Kodansha. He was co-writer of Todd McFarlane's *The Crow*, and has had several short comics published by *Vertigo/DC Comics* and by *Marvel*. He also appeared in the film *Once Upon a Time in China and America* starring Jet Li, which led him to a fruitful collaboration with its director, Sammo Hung (star of the television series *Martial Law*) writing movie treatments.

Doug Allen, also a graduate of the Rhode Island School of Design, is a co-creator of *Jickett's Speed Shop*, as well as a myriad of other illustrated stories. His humorous and always lively illustrations have appeared in *The New Yorker*, *Raw*, *Details*, *Spin*, and *Spin Online*. He is also the creator of the much-loved comic strip *Steven*, the latest incarnation of which is *Steven Out West*, a storytelling vinyl record with a read-along comic book put out by Vital Cog Records.

Daniel Gray has been writing geekbooks since 1990, with a focus on design, graphics, animation, and Internet-related topics. His irreverent style and clear explanations have sold hundreds of thousands of books worldwide.

1

Everything You Learned
on Saturday Morning
is Still True

Are you a cartoon kid? Did you spend your Saturday mornings (and weekday afternoons) glued to the tube? Seeing that you have this book in your hands, there's a good chance you did. Your mom can only hope that after spending hours absorbing all of those toons, you picked up on the techniques used by the kings of animation. (It helps a lot if you can handle endless repetition, as you watch the same cartoons, over and over.)

Here's the good news. The fundamentals of animation haven't changed; the only elements that have changed are the tools. The Twinkle method applies the classic techniques of cartoon animation to Macromedia Flash. This chapter lays out the basic principles you'll need to know before launching into the Flash-specific how-tos. (You'll learn how to apply these principles in Chapter 4.)

IT AIN'T EASY

There's a common misconception that creating a cartoon should be quick and easy. Let's get that notion out of the way. The process of animation isn't quick. It isn't easy. And it isn't for wimps. You can't simply push a button and expect jolly stuff to roll down the chute.

You have to work at it.

Consider a typical conventionally animated six-minute Bugs Bunny cartoon. Film runs at twenty-four frames per second. Assuming the cartoon was entirely animated *on twos*—meaning that there was one drawing for every two frames, or twelve drawings per second—that's 720 drawings per minute, and 4,320 drawings per eight-minute short.

That's a whole lot of drawings. The next time you start moaning about having to add yet another keyframe in Flash, just remember all those drawings you *don't* have to do.

Not All Cartoons Are Created Equal

When this book discusses non-Flash cartoons, it's most often referring to cartoons that weren't made for television. In fact, it usually means cartoons that were made before television was invented—classic cartoons created by Disney (*Snow White*, *Pinocchio*, and *Bambi*, and others of the era); the Fleischer Brothers (*Betty Boop* and *Superman*); and the Warner Brothers shorts made by Chuck Jones, Tex Avery, and Bob Clampett.

Some great animation has been produced recently (*The Iron Giant*, *The Emperor's New Groove*, *Chicken Run*, *Princess Mononoke*, the Pixar films and *Spongebob Squarepants* come to mind), and we dig that too. But generally speaking, we're talking about the classics.

Moving Stuff Around *is not* Animation

Let's say it again. Making cartoons with solid character animation is neither quick nor easy. Of course, if you just want to move stuff around on the screen, you can do that in a few minutes. You can then have some business cards made that say you're an animator, hang out your shingle, and wait for the business to not roll in.

It cannot be stressed enough that *moving stuff around the screen is not animation*. Anyone can do that, and who cares about what *anyone* can do? Animation is about *bringing characters to life*—characters that feel, think, act, and react. With any luck, those characters will, in turn, make your audience feel, think, act, and react.

Have you ever watched a Flash cartoon and said, "Well, it was pretty good *for a Flash cartoon*"? Probably.

Have you ever watched a Bugs Bunny cartoon and said, "Well, it was pretty good *for a Bugs Bunny cartoon?*" Probably not.

It's time to raise the bar. Bugs Bunny is held up to a quality standard set forth by Disney, Warner Brothers, the Fleischers, and many others. Flash animation should be held up to that same standard. This book is here to say that "pretty good for a Flash cartoon" just isn't good enough anymore.

The Fundamentals

As a Flash animator, your life can be more frustrating than that of your conventional counterpart. Working within the Flash environment puts extra constraints upon your work. Conventional animators, for example, couldn't care less about bandwidth— they're not bound by the limitations of a file format and a delivery medium. But what we strive to do is to take those limitations and make them a style.

If you're setting out to be an animator, you'll do well if you have animation fundamentals under your belt. Maybe you've picked them up from spending all those Saturday mornings watching cartoons. (Or maybe you haven't.) In either case, there's no reason to reinvent the cartoon wheel. The fundamentals of animation have been identified, debated, studied, and used for decades.

Let's start out by summarizing these animation basics, with a Twinkle twist.

The Most Important Tool

There's one thing that's more important than a fast computer, the latest software, or whatever new howyadoin' you might come up with. The most important tool you need as an animator is observation. The ability to observe will help you uncover the details in the real world that you can then apply to your animation.

Here are a couple of examples:

- *How does a really fat guy walk?* Does he shuffle, waddle, or bounce? Is he out of breath? Do his arms swing wide to accommodate his girth?

- *What does a doughnut look like when you drop it on the floor?* Does it squish or stay circular? If it's a powdered sugar doughnut, does the powdered sugar make a cloud? If it's a sprinkle doughnut, do the sprinkles shoot off in all directions or do they stick to the chocolate? If it's a jelly doughnut, does the jelly squirt out? Where from?

Observe the details. Scrutinize. If you know what a real world action is like, you'll know what to exaggerate when you animate that action.

THE TWELVE PRINCIPLES OF CHARACTER ANIMATION

In *The Illusion of Life: Disney Animation* (a book no serious animator should be without), Frank Thomas and Ollie Johnston list the twelve principles of character animation. These were identified and developed in the 1930s at the Disney Studios, and they still apply today. We can't recommend this book enough. Read it now. You simply must.

Now that you've read *The Illusion of Life* and come back (and even if you haven't yet), let's review the concepts behind these principles—much of the book you're now holding in your hands demonstrates how to apply those principles to Flash. While Frank and Ollie explain the principles with wonderful tales of the old-school Disney animators, let's get right to the essence of each, as they relate to our world.

The Twelve Principles of Animation

1 Squash and Stretch

2 Anticipation

3 Staging

4 Straight-ahead vs. Pose-to-pose action

5 Follow-through and Overlapping action

6 Slow-in and Slow-out

7 Arcs

8 Secondary Actions

9 Timing

10 Exaggeration

11 Solid drawing

12 Appeal

In this corner…A Mooney walk cycle. For a little guy, he can really move.

Squash and Stretch

This ain't rocket science, folks. It's more like rubber ball science.

When a rubber ball hits the ground, it flattens out, bounces off the ground, and resumes its spherical shape. The harder it hits the ground, the more it flattens out, or squashes. On its way to resuming its spherical shape, the ball will elongate, or stretch. Check out Figure 1.1. Squash 'n' stretch. Pretty straightforward.

But there's a catch. The rubber ball maintains the same volume no matter how much it squashes or stretches. The ball never gets any bigger or smaller. It just gets squished into different shapes.

Figure 1.1 You might not notice *squash and stretch* while an animation is playing, but you'd miss it if it weren't there.

Get your hands on a squishy rubber ball and try this out. While it might take an awfully keen eye to see a bouncing ball squish on contact, you can always simulate the effect by simply leaning on the ball. When you apply pressure to one plane, the ball will try to expand in the other plane. In other words, squash the top and it stretches on the sides.

The same holds true for any cartoon object, unless it's specifically supposed to be rigid, like an anvil. Using squash and stretch on your characters will help give them a sense of fluidity, mass, and jolliness. Just make sure the volume stays about the same— if the volume differs, the sense of reality will suffer. This is not to

Maintain Volume!

say that your cartoons should present actions in a realistic manner. If anything, they should be *un*realistic, physically impossible, wacky actions. But they have to *feel* right.

Anticipation

Try not to think of Carly Simon. Or ketchup.

Instead, try jumping in the air without any anticipatory action. Just jump. You're not going to get too far off the ground, because you'll only be using your ankles to launch yourself (if you were standing upright to begin with). To get any kind of air at all, you'll have to swing your arms behind you, bend your knees, lean over, and then jump.

Figure 1.2 Hickory Dog gets his chicken (almost).

All that is *anticipation*—the action before the action.

Anticipation accentuates a character's action, as it directs the viewer's attention to that character. It's an action in the opposite direction that provides the momentum for the main action. There's anticipation in just about every movement you make, although it may be very small.

In the scene shown in Figure 1.2, Hickory Dog first establishes the situation, "Here little birdy." He then provides anticipation, "I'm gunna git you!" before taking action, "I got you!" Timing delivers the critical element between action and reaction. "Here little birdy."

Anticipation, Action, and Reaction

Cartoons use a simple formula, over and over:

1. Tell them that you're going to do something.
2. Do it!
3. Tell them you did it.

SUSPENSE   ACTION   REACTION

Let 'em know something's about to happen.

Staging

Although you'll be working in two dimensions, the concept of *staging* is easier to understand if you think of your characters as three-dimensional, real beings. Actually, creating characters and personalities will be easier if you think of your characters as three-dimensional, real beings.

So imagine you've got two characters. One gives the other a pie in the face. Can you picture it? Because these are three-dimensional characters, you can look at them (in your mind) from any angle. Now, what's the best way to make this pie-throwing action as clear as possible to someone else? Where do you put the characters in relation to each other as well as the viewer? That's *staging*.

Do you see the action from over the pie-thrower's shoulder? A bird's-eye view? Pie-cam? If you were making a movie with actors instead of a cartoon with drawings, these would be "where do you put the camera?" questions. There's no camera in Flash, so if you want to change the angle, you will probably have to change the drawings. In animation, planning ahead *really* counts.

In the sequence shown in Figure 1.3, the audience first sees the outside of Jickett's Speed Shop *before* Ford pulls up in his (what else?) Ford. Cut to the inside of the shop where Ford's blue Ford

Figure 1.3 Would a guy named Ford drive a Chevy?

is clearly visible over his shoulder. The sequence of shots provides the visual clues the viewer needs to place Ford.

The pioneers of animation studied vaudeville performers and silent film greats—such as Charlie Chaplin, Buster Keaton, and Harold Lloyd—to see how they communicated ideas and actions to a crowd. These performers knew that *how* you show an action is just as important as the action itself.

A strong silhouette is of critical importance. If an action can be understood through the outline of the character, the action will be enhanced by the details in the character instead of relying on them. This is especially relevant in web delivery where you don't always have control over the size of the movie.

Influences

The best Flash cartoons are influenced by everything *but* other Flash cartoons. If all you're putting into your Flash cartoon is what you've seen in other Flash cartoons, your Flash cartoon will just be more of the same. Sure, you should study the cartoon classics; but how about using a camera angle you saw in a Hitchcock film? Or a setting you read about in a novel? Or better yet, something you actually experienced? The more influences you have in your mental database, the more you can squeeze into your cartoon.

Straight-Ahead vs. Pose-to-Pose Action

The straight-ahead and pose-to-pose methods present distinctly different approaches to animation.

With the *straight-ahead* method, you'll make up the action as you go along. While this lends itself to spontaneity, you some-

Straight Ahead!

times run into the "now what?" problem, or worse yet, the "what the heck is this scene about anyway?" problem.

The *pose-to-pose* method relies upon setting key poses for the character to "hit" at critical timing points (as shown in Figure 1.4) and then creating the jolliest possible transitions between those poses. This lends itself to careful choreography and, more importantly, allows you to check the timing of your character's actions; but makes it difficult to be as spontaneous.

The best bet is to do a little of both. Have a game plan (at least a start and a finish pose), start clicking, and see what happens.

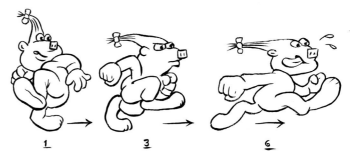

Figure 1.4 A pose-to-pose start.

Follow-Through and Overlapping Action

A batter doesn't stop swinging at the point contact is made with the baseball. A boxer doesn't freeze at the moment a punch lands. Instead, there's follow-through as the bat or glove follows its path after the primary action has occurred (the ball getting hit, or the opponent getting punched).

Wait a minute. Those are sports examples. Okay, when Moe slaps Curly, does his hand stop on Curly's cheek? No. Moe's hand hits Curly's face with enough force to turn his head, and keeps going. Moe's hand does the follow-through. Curly's head turns, then his body, then his arms—overlapping action.

The principles of *follow-through* and *overlapping action* address a single point: you should avoid stopping everything all at once. No more columns of keyframes—break 'em up! If things do come to a grinding halt, it should be for a funny moment.

When characters come to a stop, you'll want to make sure that not everything stops at once. There should be some continuance of motion, something to keep life in the scene. Take a look at the keyframes in Hickory Dog's ear (as shown in Figure 1.5)— the ear continues to sway back and forth after the rest of his body stops moving. Figure 1.6 shows the full impact, complete with follow-through.

The Moving Hold

People never stand completely still. Not even mimes. They're always moving. It could be a shift in weight, a foot tap, or plain old breathing. Frank and Ollie refer to this technique as the *moving hold*. It sounds like an oxymoron, but the idea is that even in a held pose, there's still some movement ... a little something to keep your character alive.

Figure 1.5 Hickory's flea-bitten ear just keeps on a flapping.

Figure 1.6
Hickory Dog gets hit upside the head.

Slow-in and Slow-out

It's time to get out that rubber ball again.

Throw the ball up in the air a few times and watch it carefully. Notice that the ball slows down as it reaches its peak, and speeds up as it falls (just like Hickory Dog's bouncing nose, shown in Figure 1.7). You don't need to take a class in physics to know that's gravity at work. (Remember that business about 32 feet per second squared?)

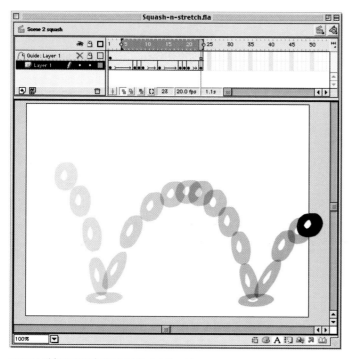

Figure 1.7 Hickory Dog's bouncing nose in onion skin.

Have you ever been on a boat (or watched from the shoreline) as it came into port? On most vessels, the captain slows the boat as it approaches the dock. It's hardly ever steady-as-she-goes right up to the dock and then a dead stop.

The principles of *slow-in* and *slow-out*—known as *easing* in Flash—are not just about starting from a standstill or coming to a stop, although that's when it's usually most noticeable. You should use easing nearly every time you tween in Flash. (If you want to jump ahead, Chapter 4 dives into the topic of easing.)

Arcs

The best things in life have curves. The same goes for animation.

The principle of *arcs* tells us that nearly everything moves in an arc, as opposed to a straight line. Try watching yourself in the mirror as you turn your head from one side to the other (or better yet, watch someone else do it). Notice that your head dips slightly at the center. Now turn your head from one side to the other, but try to keep your head completely level. Notice how much more effort this takes, and how unnatural it feels—unless you're a robot (or happen to have a really stiff neck).

This principle applies to living things, as well as non-animate objects. Move any one of your limbs and watch how it pivots— in an arc—upon the joint that anchors it to the rest of your body. Grab that rubber ball again and throw it around some more. Does it fly or bounce in a perfectly straight line?

Computers love to do things in straight lines, so it takes some effort to defeat this. If you simply set a motion tween in Flash, you'll end up with an unconvincing (and linear movement). Instead, you'll want to either use Motion Guides (as shown in Figure 1.8) or multiple keyframes to deliver a convincingly fluid movement.

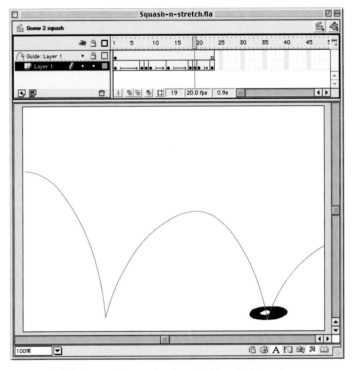

Figure 1.8 The Guide layer provides a series of arcs for Hickory Dog's bouncing nose.

Secondary Actions

It's not just the piece of fish they slap on your plate. It's the garnishes that make the presentation.

Secondary actions are smaller actions that take place while a main action occurs. This might be a bit of bouncing hair during a walk, or Hickory Dog's waving ear and tail, as shown in Figure 1.9. When Moe slaps Curly, do his cheeks jiggle? The slap is the primary action; the jiggling cheeks are the secondary actions.

Figure 1.9 Hickory Dog's walk uses subtle secondary action on the ear and tail.

Secondary actions should add to the main action, not distract. This goes back to the principle of staging. If secondary actions become too prominent, they become primary actions themselves, and may subsequently perplex the viewer. Good character animation communicates clearly with the audience. If the audience thinks, "Now what the heck is supposed to be going on here?" that's bad.

Keyframes galore.

Timing

It's all in the *timing!* Well, maybe not all, but … it's what pulls everything together.

The number of frames between key poses impacts the overall feel of the movement. The more frames you use, the slower the action; the fewer, the faster. You need to find the right balance between allowing the action to register and boring your audience.

Chuck Jones knew exactly how many frames Wile E. Coyote had to hang in the air staring at the audience, and exactly how many frames he had to fall before he hit the desert floor for maximum funniness. One frame more, or one frame less, and it just wasn't as funny.

Generally speaking, *fast is funny*. When in doubt, go faster.

If you've got a pause before a funny moment, that funny moment should go fast. It's the juxtaposition that makes it funny. Slow and slow is (usually) not funny. Fast and fast is (usually) not funny. Slow and fast, or fast and slow—now you're talkin'. It's all in the timing.

In the scene shown in Figure 1.10, Jicketts and Mooney are working when Ford comes in and interrupts them. (The scene is shot from Ford's point of view.) Jicketts looks at Ford, pauses, and then drops Mooney. The pause has to last long enough to register to the audience. When Jicketts drops Mooney, Mooney doesn't hang in the air and then fall—that's a different joke. Mooney falls fast while Jicketts holds his pose. Once that registers, Jicketts starts talking. Slow and fast juxtaposed makes for funny actions. But that same kind of timing can be used to accentuate dramatic, action-packed, or emotional scenes. It's not always about being funny. But like the man said, "Comedy is drama with timing."

Figure 1.10 Q: How long is the pause between the instant when Jicketts notices Ford and when Jicketts drops Mooney? A: Just long enough to be funny.

Most Flash cartoons are just too darn slow. Perhaps because fewer drawings are needed to make Flash animation, many Flash animators want to linger over them, and subsequently you get long, drawn out, uninteresting actions. Traditional animators realize that each drawing will be seen for a fraction of a second, and don't get too attached to them. The overall action is what counts.

Exaggeration

"Would you quit exaggerating already?"

That's one thing you won't hear one animator say to another (too often). Cartoons are all about *exaggeration*. This isn't a subtle medium. You need to make your point clearly. Exaggeration is positively the most incredibly super-spectacular way to drive your point home at a million miles an hour, baby!

When in doubt, go farther. Push that envelope. When you're setting your key poses, the characters can look ridiculous (and they probably should). But remember that you'll be seeing them for just a fraction of a second, and that exaggeration can really add to the action.

In the commentary to *The Emperor's New Groove*, director Mark Dindal says, "I like to take the approach of making some bold choices because things fail more often from not going far enough than from going too far." We couldn't agree more.

Nonetheless, poor ol' Hickory Dog suffers with that darn rock once again in Figure 1.11. Check out the exaggeration at the bottom (squash) and top (stretch) of this gag.

Solid Drawing

Solid cartoons start with *solid drawing*. You must deliver a certain level of believability, rather than fall prey to the sirens of pure gimmick and style. Cartoons, by nature, are not realistic (see Figure 1.12), but the good ones are based on reality and take it from there.

Figure 1.12
Solid drawing, man!

Figure 1.11 Should you exaggerate your stretch and squash? Why of course!

The principle of solid drawing is absolutely critical in traditional animation, but less so in Flash. That's because in traditional animation, there's a new drawing of a character every frame, and the character can't look different from frame to frame. Flash cartoons can be made with very few drawings, but those drawings have to count—thus the concept still applies.

The mechanics of Flash allow for the division of labor. Thankfully, great Flash animators needn't be great illustrators. But they do need to know what makes a drawing work within an animation. And they need to be able to communicate—to the illustrator—the exact images and poses necessary to complete a scene.

You must start with a strong drawing—one that coveys solid form—before you begin the animation process. To that end, Gary explains everything he knows about drawing in the next chapter.

Watch Out for (evil) Twins

When you draw your cartoon characters, they'll likely have two (or more) of each appendage: two arms, two legs, two eyes, two ears, and so on. Here lies a common trap for the Flash cartoonist.

You must resist the temptation to symbolize and use each appendage without altering each instance. Your character will appear flat if you use two ears, for example, at the exact same size. To avoid this, use a little scaling and rotation to gain the benefits of symbolization while adding to the character's believability. And don't forget tinting.

Appeal

"While a live actor has charisma, the animated drawing has appeal," wrote Frank and Ollie.

Your characters must ooze appeal. This works for heroes and villains alike. Even if you don't *like* the character, you should at least not mind looking at them.

Take a gander at Angel from *Jickett's Speed Shop* in Figure 1.13. Her appeal is pretty obvious. You can't help but look at her. The same goes for Tinkerbell or Red Hot Riding Hood, or any well-designed character for that matter.

We've all seen cartoons that were poorly drawn (there's plenty of them on the Internet), and maybe they've got a super *hi*-larious gag in them. But they're just no good to look at. That's a really bad thing in a visual medium. If the characters aren't appealing, you don't stand much chance of telling a compelling story with them.

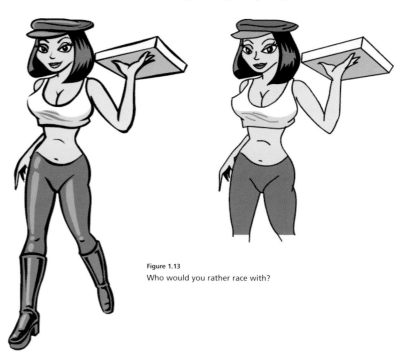

Figure 1.13
Who would you rather race with?

The problem is *South Park*. There's nothing wrong with the actual show, mind you. The problem is that *South Park* put many people under the impression that all you need to make a laugh-a-minute animation is cartoon characters who barely move but swear a lot. Who cares how well they're drawn? Who cares how well they're animated? They're kids swearing, and that's funny, right?

Well ...

That was the whole point of *South Park*. The cartoon is *intentionally* badly drawn and animated (using very sophisticated CGI software, no less). That's part of the joke. But it's a joke that can only be told once, so stop trying to tell that one. We've heard it before.

All Hail Preston Blair

Generations of budding animators got their start with the help of two remarkable books written and illustrated by the late Preston Blair. What Preston penned half a century ago still holds true today. If you really want to learn how to bring characters to life, you'll do well to learn from the master.

The two original books, *Animation* and *How To Draw Film Cartoons* are currently available as a single volume, *Cartoon Animation*, published by Walter Foster. It's not a cop out to ask you to pick up this book. Preston has laid out all the fundamentals of traditional animation. The better you understand the fundamentals, the better you can translate that to Flash.

While the most recent edition lacks the funky oversized charm of the original books, it's still a treasure—inexpensive and easily found to boot. It's a must have.

CLASS DISMISSED!

There you have it—the very basics of character animation. The successful application of these principles spells much of the difference between the wannabes and the kings and queens of the online cartoon world. Where to go to from here, you ask? Understanding great drawing is the next step, and ta da, the next chapter.

2

Drawing is a Funny Business

Regardless of how much techno-know-how you have, a successful animation must begin with a solid drawing of an engaging character. Your animated "film" will rely on the key drawings to tell the story. As you'll learn in the following chapters, creating a digital puppet out of generic anatomy does not work because it's impossible to attain the best, most specific (funniest, saddest, CRAZIEST) pose that communicates what you are trying to say. Success with the digital puppet approach requires old-fashioned cartooning values as well as the application of traditional animation techniques to Macromedia Flash. Cutting up a good cartoon is the only way to get anywhere with the methods presented in this book.

DON'T GROW UP

Children just naturally draw wacky and wild characters; however, maintaining this sense of whimsy into adulthood is frequently best left to professional idiots (er, cartoonists). The majority of dedicated cartoonists started doodling and sketching at a young age, and they have never stopped.

The early school years of most cartoonists are spent filling the margins of countless textbooks with monsters, idiots, and flipbook

animations. The crazy morons that dribbled out of our pens and pencils absorbed our attention; attention that had strayed from the math class in progress.

Divide and Conquer

If you can't draw the characters yourself, find yourself an artist with whom to collaborate. Even if modern tools allow an individual to function like an entire studio, not all Flash animators need to draw. Divide and conquer is the best way to go for the drawing-challenged among us. Keep in mind the goal here: to communicate to your audience. If the animator is working with an artist, they must get all the drawings required to tell the tale and create the action. Don't think you can rely on software tricks to replace a missing or incorrect drawing, or get the poses you need to deliver the action. Shape tweens are not a panacea.

Starting with hand-drawn artwork, the production process can be broken down into these basic steps:

Illustration As stated previously and at all costs, get the drawings you need from your artist.

Scanning If you find this task really boring (and you probably will), find someone else to do the grunt work. At Twinkle, line art is scanned in at 600 dpi as a black-and-white document. (Line art scans are often referred to as bitmap or 1-bit scans. The pixels are either on or off.) You'll want to avoid using grayscale mode or any anti-aliasing when you go from raster art to vectors. Anti-aliasing introduces ambiguity to line art; this should be avoided.

Vectorization Using Adobe Streamline, or a similar package, trace the black and white raster art into vector art that imports happily into Flash.

Dismemberment Here's where you get into the gory details. The following chapters provide detail on how to cut up the drawings to best suit the medium.

Colorization Build yourself a custom color palette, if you want consistency and a smoother workflow. While Flash's default palette consists of the 216 web-safe colors, you'll need just a handful of colors for your cartoon. By weeding out the unnecessary colors, you'll be able to colorize the vector artwork in a much more expedient fashion.

Animation Here's where the real man and woman's work begins. With your digital puppet clipped and colored, you're ready to bring life to those inanimate objects. Dr. Frankenstein has nothing on you!

Depending on how it was created, work that starts in digital vector form may jump right into the dismemberment phase.

Live for the Pain

For the confident Flash cartoonists among us, frustration is the first step in the right direction. This is not an easy medium. As long as you can laugh at yourself as you struggle to create, the "pain" involved in laying down your idea graphically will be easier to take. Remember there is nothing new about the frustration an artist feels when faced with a blank page. Nevertheless, the process of making your animation should not be a tedious drag.

In this corner...Hickory Dog demonstrates the fast run.

Consult the Masters

Know those who have gone before you and shamelessly steal from their hard-earned expertise. Watch the classics for inspirational character design. Know the work of pioneers such as Windsor McCay and Ub Iwerks. Who are these folks? Windsor McCay's landmark 1914 cartoon, *Gertie the Dinosaur,* paved the road for all to follow. Ub Iwerks developed and animated Mickey Mouse with Walt Disney, and trained many of Disney's animators. You'll do well to check out the old classic Walt Disney films.

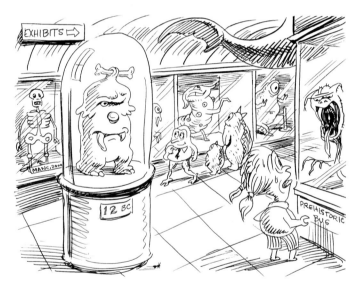

Bob Clampett, Chuck Jones, and Walt Kelley are gurus of character design. Mr. Clampett directed many Warner Brothers cartoons in the '30s and '40s, elevating Daffy Duck to star status, and went on to create Beany and Cecil. Chuck Jones created the Road Runner, Wile E. Coyote, Marvin the Martian, and Pepe Le Pew characters—in addition to contributing to the earlier "creation and/or development" of Bugs Bunny, Daffy Duck, Elmer Fudd,

and Porky Pig. Once a Disney animator, Walt Kelley is best known for his newspaper comic strip, Pogo.

Be familiar with the famed "limited" animation drawing style of UPA (United Productions of America) Pictures. The UPA studio produced Mr. Magoo and Gerald McBoing Boing, among others. Research these artists and then adapt their techniques to your needs.

While it can be difficult to find these early cartoons at your local video store, all is not lost. You'll want to scour the online stores for classic cartoons, and watch the Cartoon Network, which sometimes runs the great old stuff late at night.

Have an Idea (PLEASE)

No artist goes into this alone. We walk on the shoulders of cartooning giants; they can provide you with the craft. You have to bring that expertise and those techniques to the service of an idea; for the idea, you are on your own.

It's easy to forget the art of communication when struggling to learn a software program. Have a good idea for your animation going in, as Flash cannot make you witty or interesting. The techniques exist to tell a story. All the steps outlined in this book presume they are at the service of an idea that needs communicating. This is the animator's responsibility, and that's *you*, bub.

Armed with your idea, whether it be a story, a joke, or whatever, the support is out there to help give it form. All the resources you need are at the art museum, bookstore, library, or web portal near you. Check out the CD, as well as www.geekbooks.com for links to some of the best resources on the Internet, in addition to reviews of books, DVDs, and videos.

Your Studio

Your studio is where you live and create. It should enable as oppose to hinder the creative process. Surround yourself with research materials and objects that inspire. Have on hand examples of the kind of art you like (Figure 2.1), and refer to it often for inspiration.

Figure 2.1 Gary with just a small sample of the collection at the Twinkle studio.

Strong Key Poses from Crazy Drawings

For the digital puppet Flash character espoused in this book, much of the work is built around a single drawing, or key pose. In a good many cases, one strong drawing can be extended into a sequence, or even an entire animation. Strong key poses provide the oomph, while taking into account the economies required for Flash animation when delivered over the web.

Line Quality and Shading

Don't be wimpy or scratchy about line quality; hairy, uncertain lines will be impossible to cut up properly for animation. Avoid crosshatching and similar flowery tricks because they translate poorly into Flash. These dogs are about as scratchy as you'll want to get.

Keep a sketchbook to develop confidence and empower spontaneity in your style. The more you draw, the better you'll be able to deliver a strong character with a minimum of fuss.

Backgrounds

Raster images can be used to fabulous effect when employed as background elements in Flash. Bitmaps used in this way place your piece in the visual tradition of filmed cartoons of days past. Hand-painted scenery adds warmth to the vectorized line and color of Flash that software cannot duplicate. (Chapter 7 dives back into the topic of backgrounds.)

Violations of the Normal Must be the Rule

Do not shy away from the nuttiest exaggeration. Distortion is an important word in the cartoon vocabulary. Push the boundaries as you experiment with exaggeration. This is key to any cartooning venture, and vital to the success of a key drawing.

Have Fun While Doin' It, and Others Will Have Fun Viewin' It

Try to maintain a sense of verve and fun in your drawing. This kind of energy will be communicated when your drawing comes to life as an animation. The happiest cartoonists are those who are not afraid to experiment, and are not bound by a particular style.

ENJOY YOUR WORK

If you're not happy living in Toon Town, take a hike. Find something else to do. Go sell refrigerators or deliver soda pop. The process of creating great animation should never be considered a mere job. It's a calling. And if you hear that call, you'll do well to apply the classic principles of animation to your Flash cartoons. Coming up in the next chapter, you'll learn to do just that —when the classics meet Flash.

3

Animation Basics
in Flash

Flash is a jolly program, but like any other program, it's good for some things and not so good for others. The trick is to use the right tool for the job whenever possible, and when you can't, adjust the job to fit the tool. While you *can* use Flash as a conventional cel animation program, that doesn't really play to Flash's strengths. It might not play to your own, either.

The Twinkle philosophy doesn't bow to Flash; instead, it uses techniques to help you get the most out of the program as possible. This chapter shows you some of the tricks you can use inside (the often limiting environment) of Flash. Thankfully, Macromedia has seen fit to open up the SWF file standard, so that other software developers can write their own nifty SWF files. Later on, you learn when you might put Flash aside and reach for a different box of software.

TAKE YOUR LIMITATIONS AND MAKE THEM A STYLE

Flash is good at using the same pieces over and over again (that's what the Library is all about). Once a symbol is loaded, it doesn't have to be loaded again. Whereas traditional animation involves a new drawing for each pose, 12 times per second, the best use of Flash (or at least the most efficient) seems to be puppet animation.

Why did Terry Gilliam use paper cutouts for his hilarious Monty Python's Flying Circus cartoons? Quite simply, paper cutouts were the only way he could churn out the volume of material in the time that he had to do it. Terry took those limitations and made them a style. As time went on, he had flat files full of arms, legs, heads, backgrounds, bits and pieces that he could reuse at any given moment.

Sound familiar? A flat file of paper bits and pieces in the old world equals a Library of symbols in the Flash world.

Looking for Chunks

Dig into a Monty Python DVD or two—they include a Gilliam's Flatfile special feature, which shows some of the actual pieces that Terry Gilliam used to create his animations.

DIGITAL PUPPETS

The essence of the Twinkle method is to maximize the use of a single drawing. From a single drawing, the character is dissected into separate moving parts not quite drawn and quartered, but you get the idea where you can just rip the limbs apart at their pivot points like a lobster at a New England clambake. Reassemble the puppet, pass the drawn butter, and you're done. (If only it were that easy.)

Here's how the Twinkle method came to be.

Let's start out by saying that it helps to have a lot of art to play with. Gary Leib and Doug Allen draw constantly, on anything available (most frequently on important documents). By the time this Flash thing rolled around, Gary and Doug had accumulated about a thousand sketchbooks between them, each filled to the margins with millions of drawings of idiots. There had to be some way to squeeze some amusement out of all of those idiots; surely there must be a way to create nifty vector animation. Over time, this basic methodology appeared:

1. Scan the original art (at a resolution high enough to maintain the integrity of the original drawing).
2. Convert the bitmap scan to vectors in Adobe Streamline and save in Adobe Illustrator format.
3. Bring the (now) vector artwork into Flash.
4. Cut out the parts that need to move.
5. Fill in the blanks.
6. Move the pieces around.

That was basically it. While the method wasn't earth shattering at the time it did speak to one of the biggest problems plaguing Flash cartoons: the lack of soul. Most cartoons drawn directly in Flash lack character (an important aspect in character animation, mind you) *because the uniform outlines are too generic, without any line quality, whatsoever.*

Chapter 2 hammered down the gospel: It all starts with the drawing. It can be just about anything, but some drawings lend themselves to animation better than others because they immediately suggest an action. And animation means action—specific action. In the upper-left corner of every left-facing page of this book there's a goofy drawing by Gary or Doug. When you find one that makes you laugh, or suggests a specific action, ask yourself:

• What's going on in this drawing?
• What can I make this character do?

Of course you can draw straight in Flash. You can even draw the pieces you need in advance; but then you lose the spontaneity of an amusing drawing. If a static drawing makes you laugh, chances are it'll keep making you laugh when it moves. You may also find it difficult to get a specific pose or gesture, versus drawing the exact pose you need, and then animating into and out of that pose.

So enough with the theory already! Let's pick an idiot and do something with it. The li'l robot shown in Figure 3.1 seems pretty jolly. Let's start with her.

Figure 3.1
Yeah, it's a one-legged robot. You got a problem with that?

Scanning For Flash

While Flash can incorporate both bitmap and vector artwork, it's happiest when animating vector objects. While some Flash purists scream "vector vector vector," the Twinkle method uses a mix of vectors and bitmaps—primarily vectors for animated characters and props, with bitmaps for backgrounds. Because most of the artwork around here consists of hand-drawn originals, the scanner gets a workout. Once the characters and props have been scanned, those drawings are converted to vectors.

It's best to use a high-resolution bitmap scan. The resolution, of course, depends on the size of the original. In this case, the drawing was scanned in at 150%, 600 ppi, because the drawing was pretty small to begin with. Streamline or Flash should have plenty of data to work with when the image is converted to vectors. While a certain amount of bastardization (or "stylization," if you prefer) is inherent in vectorizing, Twinkle prefers to keep the drawing looking like a drawing. If that means more vector points, so be it.

Twinkle uses Adobe Streamline primarily, but you can vectorize your artwork any way you want, as long as the end result looks good, as does the vectorized robot in Figure 3.2. (Of course, if you don't own a copy of Streamline, you can always use the Modify > Trace Bitmap command in Flash.) When in doubt, opt for more detail. You can always optimize it down later.

Looking for Art?

The art files for this exercise can be found in the Chapter 3 folder on this book's CD-ROM. The original scan file is named robotscan.tif (Figure 3.1), while the Streamlined file is named robotvectors.ai (Figure 3.2).

Figure 3.2
It's not just the devil in the details (it's the integrity of the artwork, too).

Clean Up and Color

Once you've used Streamline to vectorize the robot file, save it and import it into Flash (Cmd/Ctrl+R). Once the robot is imported, she should look something like Figure 3.3. Make sure everything is selected, and break it apart (Cmd/Ctrl+B), and you end up with a robot that resembles Figure 3.4.

Figure 3.3 The robot as imported into Flash.   Figure 3.4 All broken up.

Now that the robot has been broken into bits, you can color it and "make it nice." It's sometimes helpful to change the background color so you can see if any areas have no fill; otherwise, the artwork will be all black and white (and it can be difficult to see which areas are open and which are not). Select Modify > Movie and then change the background color to something you know you won't be using, as shown in Figure 3.5.

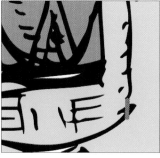

Figure 3.5 A lurid green is usually a safe bet.

Once you've altered the background color, it's easy to spot the white chunks, as demonstrated by Figure 3.6.

Figure 3.6
White chunks will stick out like, well, like white chunks.

Try not to rely too heavily on the Paint Bucket's gap-closing feature. Instead, use the Line tool to temporarily close the gaps, as shown in Figure 3.7. While this can take a little more time, it may be worth it. Look closely at Figure 3.8 and you see one effect of coloring artwork on autopilot: little chunks without color. Use a steel gray (#669999) to fill in the robot.

Figure 3.7 Close that gap!

Figure 3.8 Little areas of non-color are uncool.

Want more proof? Figure 3.9 provides another demonstration of errant gap closing, while Figure 3.10 shows a properly filled area (created with a temporary line).

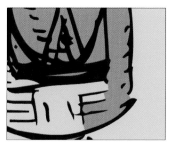

Figure 3.9 Bad! The Paint Bucket doesn't always draw the line in the right place.

Figure 3.10 Good! Draw a temporary line before filling and you'll have more control over the Paint Bucket.

Does this mean you should never use the Close Gap feature? Why of course not! Sometimes it's a godsend. Try it, see how it looks, and if it isn't right, do it by hand. Being the discerning animator, surely you prefer a hand-drawn appearance, as opposed to the computer-manufactured variety.

When you're done, be sure to double-click on the temp line to select it and then delete it. It also helps to connect these lines when possible, so they all get selected at once when you're ready to delete, as shown in Figure 3.11.

Figure 3.11
Delete 'em when
you're done.

Done coloring? Don't forget to paint in the fun stuff—those little flat color highlights (#66CCCC), shadows (#006666), and accents (#99CCCC) that really make it snappy. (Figures 3.12 and 3.13 show before and after views.) Flat color highlights are preferred over the more generic gradient. Gradients are fine, but should be used sparingly. It's surprisingly difficult to use a gradient well, and besides, they're processor-intensive.

Figure 3.12 The bot before highlights, shadows, and accents.

Figure 3.13 Highlights, shadows, and accents applied.

Gradients: Use Only as Directed

Hey, we've all seen cases of gradients gone bad. Ready for the good stuff? Check out the books of J. Otto Seibold ("Mr. Lunch", "Olive the Other Reindeer", and "Monkey Business" to name a few) and you'll see gradients used to great effect.

Save the file as robot.fla before proceeding to the next section.

Building the Digital Puppet

Okay, Gepetto. It's time to make the puppet—but first you must dismember the drawing. What sort of action is this wacky little robot capable of? How about jumping? The robot will consist of three basic pieces: the head, the leg, and the foot. You need to cut out the pieces, fill in the blanks, make them symbols, and put it back together. Let's start with the head.

Using the Arrow or the Lasso tool, select the head. Copy the head, make a new layer, and use Edit > Paste In Place to paste the head in the exact same position (on the new layer). Rename the new layer something descriptive (how about "head"?), as shown in Figure 3.14; then lock and hide the original layer.

Figure 3.14
The bot has sprouted a new head on its own layer.

Dismember with Care

Now, you need to select and delete anything that isn't part of the head. When possible, click on isolated chunks with the Arrow tool, and then delete them, rather than use the Eraser tool. Figure 3.15 shows a piece of the leg hanging below the robot's chin, as well as a couple of accent lines at the lower left.

Figure 3.15
You want to get rid of that extra stuff.

Once the isolated chunks are gone, use the Eraser tool to carve the edge of the robot's chin, as shown in Figure 3.16. You can then select the remaining chunk with the Arrow tool, and delete.

Figure 3.16
Use the Eraser tool to define the line.

Now erase the unnecessary line art. If you're worried about the extra curves the Eraser tool will cause, you can again use the temporary line technique in a manner similar to that shown previously in Figures 3.10 and 3.11.

Symbolize and Position

It's preferable to work with groups rather than ungrouped chunks. Group the head (Cmd/Ctrl+G), and make it a symbol (F8). Name the symbol something descriptive (something like "head"). Flash will automatically center the head in the symbol, as shown in Figure 3.17.

Figure 3.17
By default, the head's center point is directly between the eyes; however, that's not where you want it to pivot.

Any translation, such as scaling or rotation, will be oriented at the center; this will almost always need to be changed. The center point of the symbol should be where the piece would naturally pivot if it were part of a real object. In this case, the head would pivot at the neck. Double-click the symbol to open it up and then move the head upward so the center point is about where the neck would be, as shown in Figure 3.18.

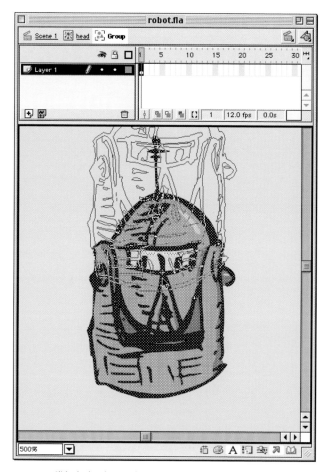

Figure 3.18   Slide the head upward, so that the center point is just above the chin.

Naming Conventions

Be kind to yourself and your cohorts. Come up with (and stick to) a solid set of naming conventions for your symbols, layers and scenes, and you can stay sane. Take a look at this pair of Libraries of Ford poses. The first (evil) Library shows what *not* to do; it's inconsistent and confusing. You wouldn't want to look at that mess on a morning after a hard night on the town.

The second (good) Library, on the other hand, demonstrates proper methodology. Each symbol is explicitly named, following a set hierarchy. With just a glance, you can see that all of the symbols are part of FordWalk. You can immediate identify each symbol, whether it's part of a limb or the complete cycle. But beware the capitals! To Flash, "Arm-Zinger" comes before "arm-arugala". Flash puts capital letters ahead of lower case letters alphabetically. Live with it.

Now return to the Scene and view the original layer. Whoops … the head's moved because the symbol's center point has been changed, as shown in Figure 3.19.

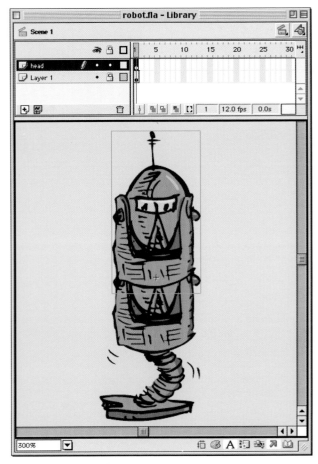

Figure 3.19 Looks like she's lost her head.

You need to move the head back into position. While you can eyeball it, you should try to be as precise as possible. It's helpful to switch to Outline mode (View > Outline) and then zoom in, so you can line up the symbol exactly with the original. Figures 3.20 and 3.21 show the bot in outline mode.

Respect that art!

Figure 3.20 Okay, so now you have a good reason to pick some new layer colors.

TIP Edit Center is not the same thing as changing the center in the Symbol. Edit Center adjusts the center only for the current transform.

Figure 3.21
The bot's head,
back in place.

Put Back What's Not There

Let's move on to the leg. In this case, you have to fill in some blanks. Repeat the procedure you used for the head: Copy the leg, use Paste In Place on a new layer (name it "leg"), and erase the unnecessary chunks, as shown (mid-process) in Figure 3.22.

Figure 3.22
Carve carefully
and then delete
the extra chunks.

If this were a real robot, the leg would go up into the head, and attach somewhere—perhaps where you put the pivot point. You need to draw in the part that was obscured by the head in the original drawing (see Figure 3.23).

Figure 3.23
Is that a shrimp, a lawn grub, or a robot's leg?

Do your best to emulate the original line quality. You may find it easiest to manipulate the paths to get the results you want. This has the added attraction of not adding points, but simply altering existing points. The end result should look something like Figure 3.24.

Figure 3.24
Make sure you've drawn enough.

Group the leg, make it a symbol, then name it "leg," and change the center point just like you did with the head. The leg will pivot at the neck and at the ankle, so you have to pick one. In this case, go with the ankle because it's very clear where the ankle should go, but not as specific where the neck should go. Aim for the neighborhood of what you see in Figure 3.25.

Figure 3.25
Move the center point; then fiddle in Outline view to get the leg back in position.

TIP You'll have a much harder time keeping the foot connected to the ankle if the pivot is at the head, rather than keeping the head connected to the leg if the pivot is at the ankle. If this makes no sense now, you'll get it as soon as you start animating.

Now do the foot. Same deal as the neck and head. Copy the foot, create a new layer named "foot," and Paste in Place. Erase the bit of leg, and draw in the missing chunk. Group the foot, symbolize (name it "foot"), and move the pivot point to where the ankle meets the foot, as shown in Figure 3.26. You can now delete the original layer.

You should now have a robot that looks exactly like the original drawing, except it's in three animatable pieces. The layers should be in the order necessary for the symbols to properly overlap. The head should be in front of the leg, and the leg should be in front of the foot. Figure 3.27 shows your digital puppet. Save the file as robot-puppet.fla and then get ready to bring her to life.

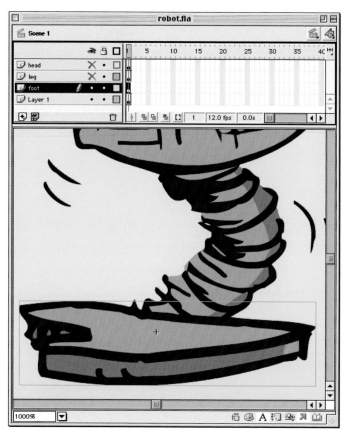

Figure 3.26 Same technique, different bot part.

Figure 3.27 Ready to animate!

ANIMATING THE PUPPET

With the robot severed into three marvelous symbols—head, leg, and foot—you're finally ready to animate. The pieces can now be transformed. How would a one-footed robot get around? Unless it can hover, it would probably have to hop around to get anywhere. To make this little robot jump, you need to put a handful of classic animation principles to use, including antici-pation, squash and stretch, follow-through, and maybe a little secondary action.

Let's go pose-to-pose on this one, because it's a single, specific action. Begin with the gross action, and gradually refine. Set a row of keyframes at frame 10 for now. This will be our end point. Select all the pieces and then move them to the left, as shown in Figure 3.28. Set a motion tween between the keyframes on every layer and play. Your robot's moving, but she's not doing too much in the way of jumping.

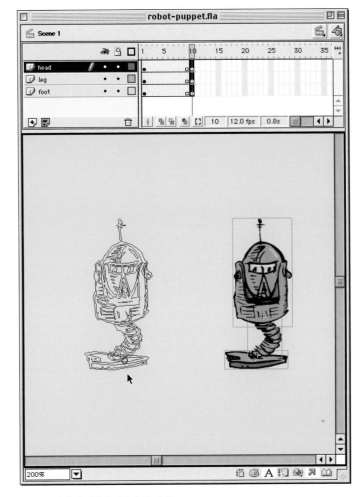

Figure 3.28 A (boring) little slide to the left.

Now set a row of keyframes at Frame 5, as shown in Figure 3.29. Move all three pieces up in the air, and play. The robot's jumping, but the motion is still unacceptable. A little anticipation will make this more believable. (Remember, anticipation is the action before the action.) Before the robot can jump up, it's got to bend down. To do this, you have to add some new keyframes.

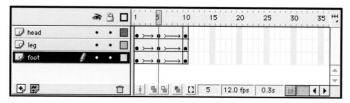

Figure 3.29   Frame 5 is the apex of the hop.

Move the playhead to Frame 3. Select the head layer, and Insert > Keyframe; then do the same for both the leg and foot layers. Copy the row of keyframes at Frame 1 by selecting Frame 1 in all three layers and then Edit > Copy Frames, and paste them into Frame 3 by selecting frame 3 in all three layers and then Edit > Paste Frames. Now do a little squash and stretch on the leg, using a Scale transform. Rotate the leg—just approximate for now— where the head will be because the layer preview is turned off in Figure 3.30. If you select the head and the leg, and rotate them both, Flash rotates around the center of the two objects. We want the leg to rotate at the ankle, where we put the center point.

Figure 3.30   Always make sure to maintain volume when you squash and stretch.

Now move the head to the top of the leg. Rotate the head so the robot is really leaning down, as shown in Figure 3.31. Exaggerate! Play it back. Getting better!

Figure 3.31   Ready, set …

Now let's do a little slow-in and slow-out. Because the robot is starting from a standstill to a movement, it's going to start slowly and then speed up. First, let's delete two frames between keyframes 5 and 10 to speed up the drop so that the final frame is 8. Select the tweens between keyframes 1 and 3, and use the Frame palette to set the easing to about −80 (ease in), as shown in Figure 3.32. As the robot reaches the apex of its jump, it'll slow down, so set the easing between keyframes 3 and 5 to 100 or so (ease out). As it falls towards the ground, it'll speed up again (that's gravity for you), so set the easing between keyframes 5 and 8 to −70 or so.

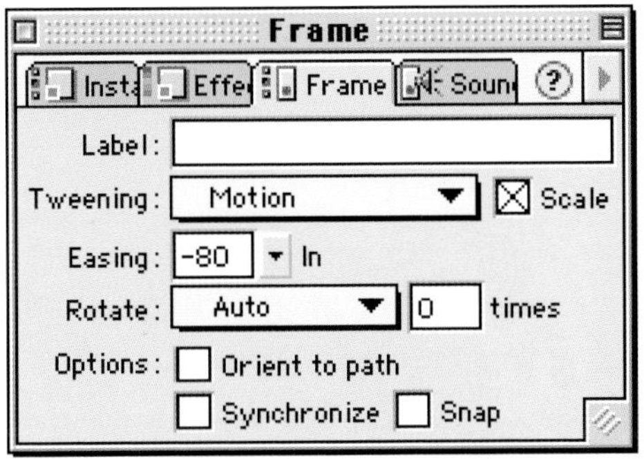

Next, adjust the easing to check the timing. If the robot's in the air too long, or not long enough, change it now. If it still appears to be taking a little too long to land; delete a frame between keyframes 5 and 8. The last row of keyframes should now be at frame 7, as shown in Figure 3.33. Play it back, and see if it looks better.

Figure 3.32
Ease in and ease out are set via the Frame palette.

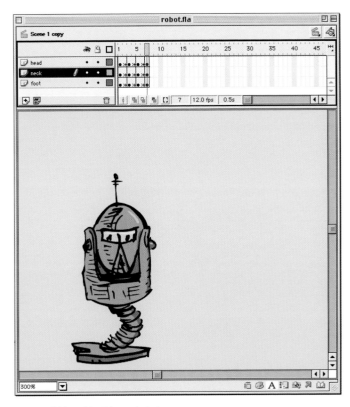

Figure 3:33 Add or subtract frames to taste.

The mid-air pose needs work. Here's where you can really add some character. Which is heavier, the head or the foot? Is jumping easy or hard for the robot? You decide, and pose it accordingly. Figures 3.34 and 3.35 give you an idea or two. Remember to squash and stretch the leg, using a Scale transform. It's best to rotate the leg and foot together; then move it to correspond with the head. This keeps the ankle locked to the foot.

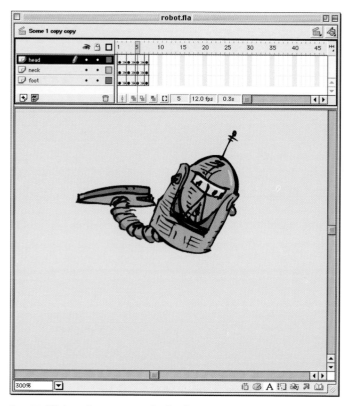

Figure 3:34 This is one happy, peppy, and springy bot!

Figure 3.35 Don't let your body parts separate.

Let's work on the landing to give the robot some weight, and the landing some impact. Set a row of keyframes at frame 9, and add tweens with an ease out. Now at frame 7, set the landing pose. How hard does the robot land? Figures 3.36 and 3.37 provide a couple of variations. Play back your version and see how it looks.

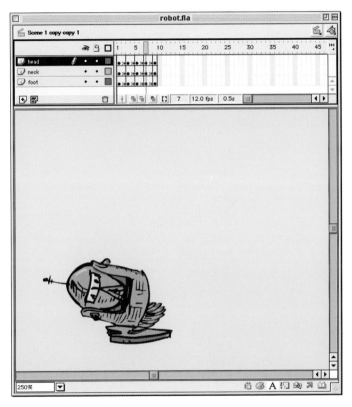

Figure 3.36 A soft (enough) landing?

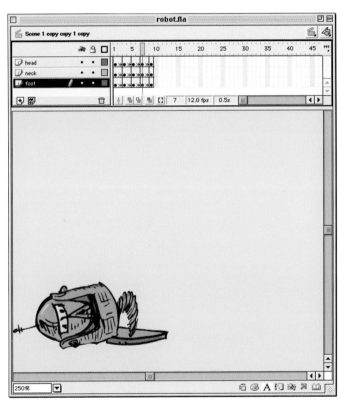

Figure 3.37 A little exaggeration never hurt a cartoon.

Not bad, but still a little stiff. That's because Flash's tweening always picks the shortest point between keyframes, not the most interesting point. (Where is that darn Make Interesting button, anyway?) So at frame 6, add another row of keyframes, and give the robot a falling pose, again taking into account how heavy the foot is. In this case, the foot will lead the robot. Turning on Onion Skin can help, as demonstrated by Figure 3.38.

Now for some finishing touches. Remember that follow-through means not everything stops at once. Right now, the foot, the leg, and the head all stop at the same time. Let's make the leg stop and then the head. Add a keyframe at frame 11 for the head, and blank frames for the other layers. Add a tween and ease out (because it's slowing to a stop). Now at frame 9, rotate the head so it overshoots the stopping point, as shown in Figure 3.39.

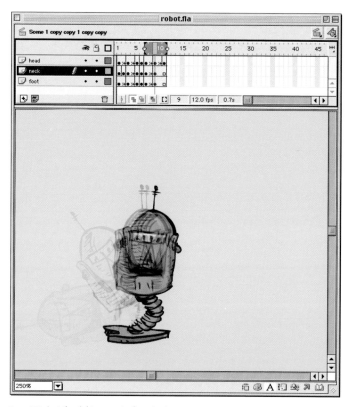

Figure 3.38 Onion Skin to get the feel for the fall. Once again, add or subtract frames to suit.

Figure 3.39 Just the right amount of sproing!

SOUND THE BELL

Done? Sure, if you're a wuss. This is just a start. The real character animation is yet to come. Depending on how much spring you want the robot to have, you could make the head bob back and forth several times after it lands. You could have it anticipate the anticipation at the very start of the jump. You could have the foot be so heavy that once in the air, the head stays put long enough to be funny and then zips down to join the rest. You can find some examples in the Chapter 3 folder on the CD, but come up with your own—the jollier the better. See how much you can do with this single drawing. You started by moving things around on the screen. Now you're bringing a character to life.

4 Principles Applied

So you've drawn a character
(or got someone to do it for you),
Streamlined it, cut it apart, and
made it into a digital puppet.
Now you're ready to really animate.
That means going back to the twelve
classic principles of animation you
learned in Chapter 1. This chapter
demonstrates how you can apply
those principles with Flash.

SLOW-IN AND SLOW-OUT (EASING)

Slow-in and slow-out are called *easing* in Flash. Ease in means starting slow and speeding up, and goes from 0 to –100. Ease out means starting fast and slowing down, and goes from 0 to 100. When Hickory Dog's nose falls to the ground, it will ease in because gravity will make it speed up as it gets closer to the ground. After it hits the ground, it will ease out—taking off quickly—as it bounces upwards. Then the nose will slow down until it runs out of steam and starts falling again. How much is a matter of taste.

Knowing whether to ease in or out and how much is mostly determined by feel. When you add easing, does the action feel more natural? A good way to tell if you're easing in the right direction is to crank it up to 100 (or –100) so the action is obvious. Once you've determined which way to ease, you can back down until it feels right.

Generally, the start of an action will ease in. It takes effort to overcome inertia, so an action will start slow and then speed up. Point your finger at something. Do it fast. Start with your hand close to your body; then snap your whole arm into the pointing position. When is your arm moving the fastest? At the start or the end of the action? Chances are it was going at maximum speed just before it came to a stop. There are, of course, many occasions when an action will start fast, but those usually fall under the "fast is funny" category, such as a sudden dash offscreen after the character realizes he's about to be eaten by a giant squid (he blinks first, pausing long enough for it to be funny, and then *zing!*)

It is not so generally true that the end of an action will ease out. The finger pointing exercise is a good example of an action that eases in but doesn't ease out (instead it overshoots—see below).

An action that slows to a stop will certainly ease out. Do the same finger pointing action, but this time immediately return your hand to the start position. Your hand should naturally ease into the point, and ease out to the end pose. The only exception might be if you're jerking your arm around (be kind to your mouse hand!).

Try to use easing every chance you get. Rarely does anything move at a constant rate, least of all characters. Easing helps take the unnatural mechanical feeling out of your animation—and it doesn't cost you anything—so use it!

Easing, however, can cause joints to slip out of place when you add keyframes for some parts and not others during a tween. That's because the extra keyframes shorten the length of the tween for that part, while the others have a longer tween; then one part is moving faster (or slower) than the other parts. So the easing in that case will have to be adjusted to keep the joints in place. If that fails, set more keyframes.

ARCS

Nearly all character movement involves arcs. Rarely do living things make movements in straight lines. Computers, however, normally do things in straight lines. The results of letting the computer do what it wants usually looks unnatural. Setting your pivot points properly will help you animate with arcs. Arms pivot at the shoulder, and that movement goes in an arc. If you set the center point of your arm symbols where it would connect to the shoulder, the arm will move in an arc when rotated.

If your character turns its head from one side to the other, be sure to make the chin dip in the middle of the turn. Watch Ford in the *Jickett's Speed Shop* pilot as he turns his head to see if the coast is clear.

Flash's motion guides help provide convincing movement, with or without arcs. Motion guides can be any shape, so you can make complex arcing motions with a single guide. You can use a motion guide to make Hickory Dog's nose bounce across the screen, or you can alter that path and make his nose get possessed by the devil.

Yet another simple but effective trick (and aren't those the best kind?) is to offset the center point. This trick only works with flying chunks that don't have to be attached to anything. For example, let's say you want to make Hickory Dog's nose fly across the screen. You could have it go in a straight line from keyframe A to keyframe B(oring). You could use a motion guide to make it nice. Or, you could have it go in a straight line from keyframe A to keyframe B with an offset center.

Making an Arc

Here's how to make a sneaky arc using an offset center and a bit of rotation. Open the arc.fla file from the CD-ROM, then:

1. Edit the Nose symbol, and move it away from the center point (using the technique used in Chapter 3), as shown in Figure 4.1
2. Put it in a scene on one side of the frame. Set a keyframe at frame 10 or so and then move the nose to the other side of the screen, as shown in Figure 4.2. Set a tween.
3. Rotate Hickory's nose, as shown in Figure 4.3.

Play it, and check out that arc. The end result should look something like Figure 4.4.

Note that the center points at both keyframes are level. This technique is useful if, for example, you need to have many blobs of melted plastic fly off a flaming telephone. That way you don't have to have a million Guide Layers—all these blobs are flying at once using just two keyframes each.

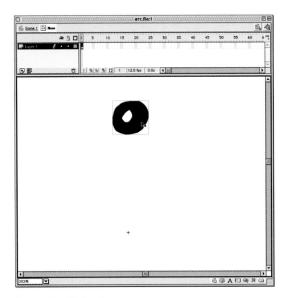

Figure 4.1 The offset center.

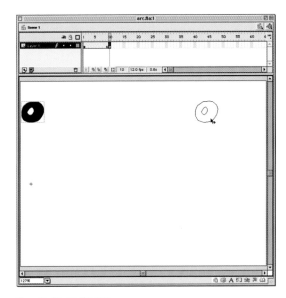

Figure 4.2 Moving the nose.

In this corner...Hickory's nose doing the classic bouncing ball routine.

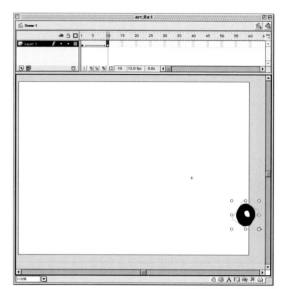

Figure 4.3 Nose rotation.

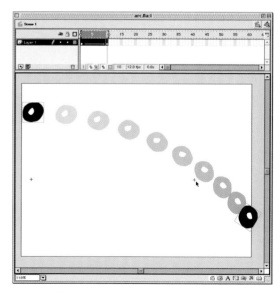

Figure 4.4 The nose in onion skin. Nice arc!

SQUASH AND STRETCH

Flash makes squash and stretch really easy, thanks to the scaling tool. It's your biggest weapon against stiffness in your animation, and it'll help you avoid the "paper cutout" look. Just because you're animating chunks as though they were paper cutouts doesn't mean they have to *look* like paper cutouts. You can't really squeeze and skew paper, now can you? And if you were doing cel animation, you'd have to account for squash and stretch in every drawing so that each one has a little more squash (or stretch) than the last.

Let's take the example of Hickory Dog's bouncing nose. You're going to have to crack open the CD and look at these files because squash and stretch (and all animation, for that matter) is a function of time. An object or character can look utterly ridiculous in a single frame. You might look at the object or character and think, "hey, that can't be right!" But as one frame of many, it can

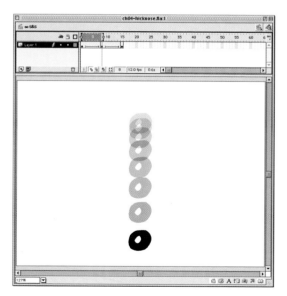

Figure 4.5 That's not a nose. That's a bowling ball.

make for jolly animation. Hickory's bouncing nose is in the file called ch04-hicknose.fla. The first scene, called "no S&S," has Hickory's nose bouncing with no squash and stretch (Figure 4.5). As you can see, it's pretty dull without squash and stretch.

Maintaining Volume

The key to successful squash and stretch is maintaining volume. If you squash, make sure you stretch. If you stretch, make sure you squash. There's always the same amount of Hickory Dog nose, whether it's flattened out or stretched thin. Watch what happens when you don't maintain volume: the size of the nose changes. Play the scene called volume on the CD and see for yourself how unacceptable it looks.

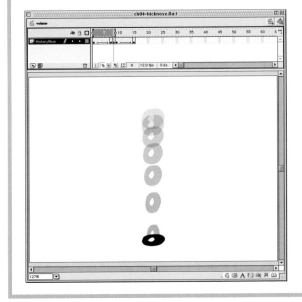

The (non) Center Point

Notice where the center point is on the nose in Figure 4.6. It's at the bottom instead of the center. When you make an object into a symbol, Flash centers it by default. This isn't always where you want the center point to be because all transformations are based around that center point.

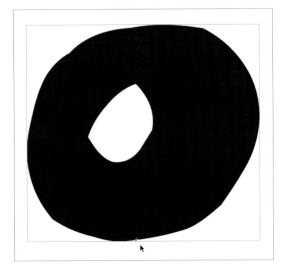

Figure 4.6 This nose is going to bounce, so the center point has been moved to the bottom.

In this case, Hickory's nose is going to hit some unspecified surface, so you'll want to draw in a guideline to show where it will hit, as shown in Figure 4.7.

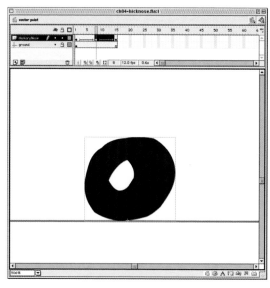

Figure 4.7 The guideline sets the [insert surface to be hit here].

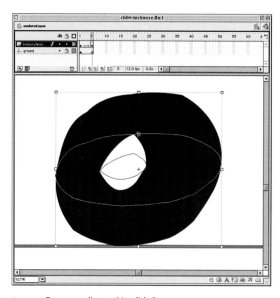

Figure 4.8 Do you smell something fishy?

If Hickory's nose symbol had its center point at the center, and some squash and stretch were applied to it, there would be extra effort involved in keeping the nose "locked" to the ground. Figure 4.8 shows the scale in process. Go to the scene called centered nose exercise in the ch04-hicknose.fla file. In the next few steps, you'll lock down that nose.

1. Go to the keyframe at frame 5, click Hickory's nose, and use the Scale tool to squash it down vertically The nose isn't on the ground anymore.

2. Now stretch the nose out horizontally, as shown in Figure 4.9. Remember to maintain volume!

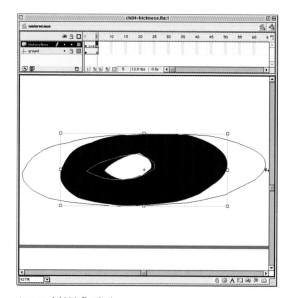

Figure 4.9 Ack! It's floating!

3. Move the nose down to touch the "ground," as shown in Figure 4.10. You can hold down the Shift key to constrain it vertically.

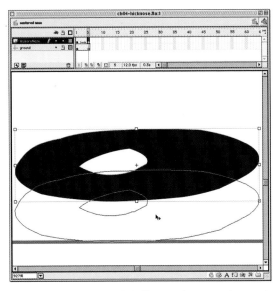

Figure 4.10 The brute force method of keeping the nose on the ground.

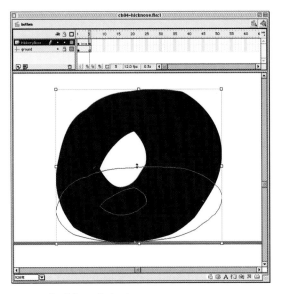

Figure 4.11 Here's the vertical scale.

Looks fine, right? In this particular example, it's not such a big deal; but as the action gets more complicated, having the center point in the right place can really make your life a lot easier and your animation a lot jollier. Try it again with the center point at the bottom of the nose this time. Go to the scene called **bottom exercise** in the **ch04-hicknose.fla** file. Let's do the squash and stretch thing again:

1. Same deal. At frame 5, vertically scale Hickory's nose, as shown in Figure 4.11. Use the corner handle at the top of the object. Whatta difference!

2. Stretch it horizontally—maintain that volume! Take a look at Figure 4.12; the nose is still locked to the ground, with no extra effort.

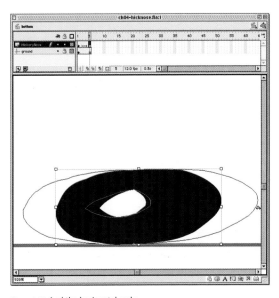

Figure 4.12 And the horizontal scale.

Now let's apply some squash and stretch to the bouncing Hickory nose to "make it nice." Go to the scene named S&S exercise in the ch04hicknose.fla file. Do the same squash and stretch you've done twice now to Hickory's nose to the keyframe at frame 8. Play it back. What's wrong with this cartoon? Figure 4.13 shows Hickory's nose flattening out *before* it hits the ground. Unacceptable! (The S&S wrong scene shows the wrong way to do it.)

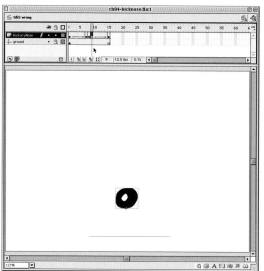

Figure 4.14 Add those keyframes.

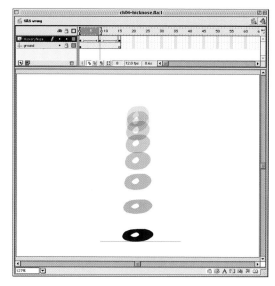

Figure 4.13 Try again, kids. Don't squash that object until it hits something.

As Hickory's nose drops, it should elongate to accentuate the speed of the fall. When it hits the ground, it should flatten out to emphasize the impact. As it rebounds back into the air, it should start out elongated (because the momentum continues), and as it slows to a stop in the air, it should regain its original shape.

Undo that squash and stretch, and let's get it right. Follow these steps:

1. Add a keyframe one frame before and one frame after the impact point, frame 8 (Figure 4.14).

2. At keyframe 7, stretch Hickory's nose out so it's nice and skinny, as shown in Figure 4.15. Don't forget to maintain volume!

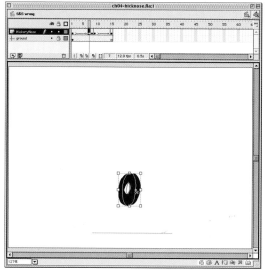

Figure 4.15 A skinny nose equals a rapidly falling nose.

3. Move the elongated nose closer the ground, as shown in Figure 4.16. How much closer is up to you. This will add extra impact to the moment when Hickory's nose hits the ground.

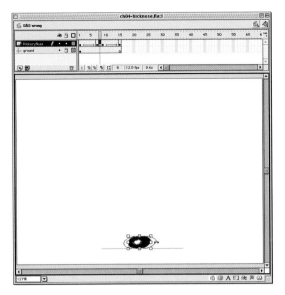

Figure 4.17 We have impact!

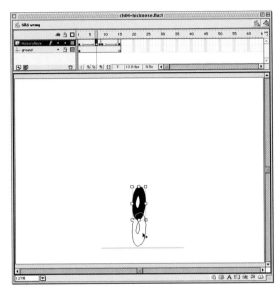

Figure 4.16 Don't let Flash tell you where to put your chunks.

4. Squash the nose at keyframe 8, as shown in Figure 4.17. You should be good at this by now. Maintain what? That's right: volume.

5. At keyframe 9, elongate the nose again, and move it closer to the ground—in a similar matter to what you did with keyframe 7. You could copy keyframe 7, but a little variation, like that shown in Figure 4.18 is less computer-y. Replace any easing that might have disappeared.

You should now have a much jollier animation than before.

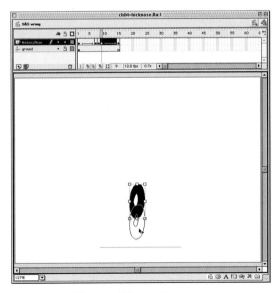

Figure 4.18 Just a little more will do the trick.

Skewing

Don't forget to make use of Flash's capability to skew symbols (another way Flash has paper chunks beat!). When you use the Rotate tool, if you grab the middle transform handles instead of the corners, it'll skew the symbol around the center point's axis. That's not so useful with Hickory's nose bouncing up and down, but it makes a big difference when Hickory's nose goes bouncing across the screen.

Open up the arc scene in the ch04-hicknose.fla file. Figure 4.19 shows Hickory's nose bouncing across the screen with no squash and stretch at all.

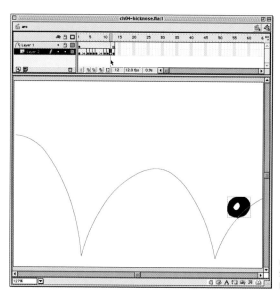

Figure 4.20
Set those
keyframes.

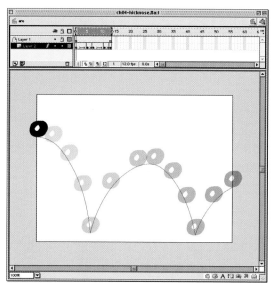

Figure 4.19
Ouch.
No squash,
no stretch.

2. Squash and stretch the nose at the impact keyframes. It can squash a little less on the second hit, if you like. Maintain volume (Figure 4.21)!

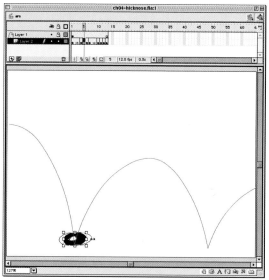

Figure 4.21
Splooosh!

You can probably extrapolate from the previous exercise how to add some squash and stretch to Hickory's nose. Let's get that nose bouncing along in an acceptable manner:

1. Set keyframes at the frames before and after each keyframe where Hickory's nose hits the ground (keyframes 5 and 11), as shown in Figure 4.20.

3. Stretch the nose before and after keyframes, and move the nose closer to the ground to give the hit some impact (Figure 4.22). Using View > Snap to Objects helps you keep the nose on the motion guide.

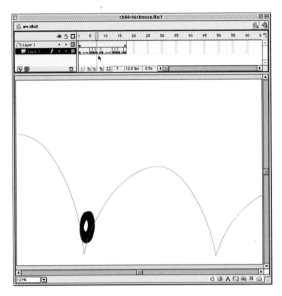

Figure 4.23 Get the timing down.

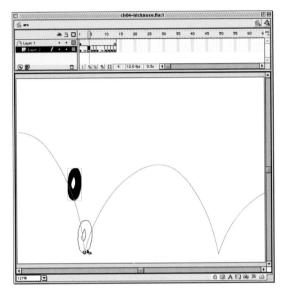

Figure 4.22 Play it again, Sam.

4. Adjust the timing as necessary (Figure 4.23). I added one frame between keys at frames 1 and 4, one frame between the keys at frames 6 and 7, and one frame between the keys at frames 12 and 13. After that, I put the easing back to 40 on the keyframe at frame 7 and 15.

5. Now make it nice. Use the rotate tool to skew Hickory's nose in the direction of the motion guide, as shown in Figure 4.24.

> **TIP** Always use the transform handles furthest from the center point. They give you the most control over your chunks.

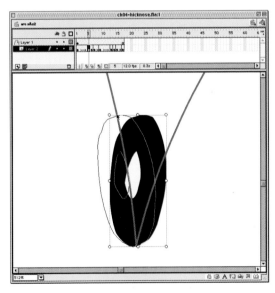

Figure 4.24 Skew to follow the arc.

6. When you're all done, the end result should resemble Figure 4.25. Try and do *that* with paper chunks.

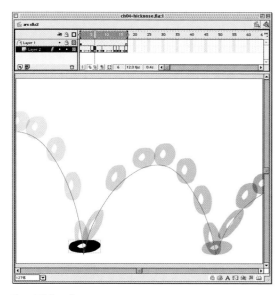

Figure 4.25 Fancy!

Squash and stretch adds a lot to your animation with little effort on your part. It works great on just about everything—even text. (Try adding a little squash and stretch to your next flying text animation!) Nearly everything squashes and stretches, unless it's supposed to be a hard, rigid object— and even then, you can do a little squash and stretch to play against expectation. But you aren't limited to squashing and stretching one symbol at a time.

Squashing and Stretching Multiple Chunks

Quick review: Everything that you're going to animate in Flash must be a symbol, and each symbol must have its own layer. In fact, everything that you use more than once should be a symbol; if you're not sure, make it a symbol anyway. It can't hurt.

Here's a typical, everyday situation for Hickory Dog. There's a big rock hovering over his head (Figure 4.26). When the rock hits him, it's definitely squash and stretch time. He will, of course, maintain his volume throughout all this squashing and stretching.

Figure 4.26 Uh oh.

Open up the ch04-squash.fla file from the CD-ROM and then select the Hick S&S exercise scene:

1. Drop the rock on Hickory's head. Put a keyframe at frame 5, and drag the rock down way past the top of his head. Add some easing (ease in to –80 or so).

2. Add a row of keyframes for each Hickory Dog part at frame 5. Select all the Hickory Dog parts at keyframe 5 and then click on the Scale tool. Do not select the rock. Lock the rock layer, if you like. Figure 4.27 shows everything ready to squash and stretch.

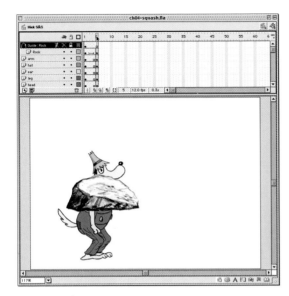

Figure 4.27 Ready to go.

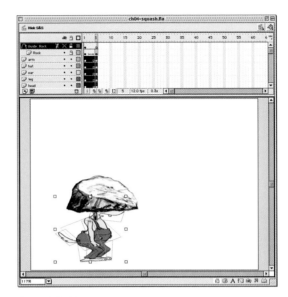

Figure 4.28 Ouch!

3. Using the top middle transform handle, scale Hickory Dog down vertically so his head is slightly behind the rock, as shown in Figure 4.28. Because you've selected multiple items, it scales around the side opposite the transform handle you use.

4. Scale Hickory horizontally to fatten him up and maintain volume, as shown in Figure 4.29. Again, you're transforming multiple items, so scale him a little on each side to keep him centered.

Having a rock dropped on his head should flatten Hickory Dog pretty good, so don't be afraid to be extreme with the squash and stretch. You'll see it only for a split-second, but it will really add impact to your animation. Depending on where you put the rock in the down keyframe, you might need to squash Hickory Dog before frame 5. In that case, set another row of keyframes at frame 4, and do a little squash and stretch.

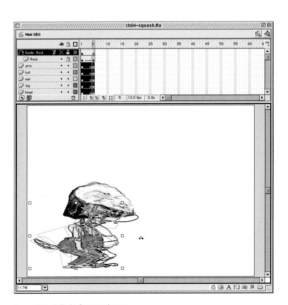

Figure 4.29 A little fatter, please.

The reason you want to squash and stretch multiple symbols all at once instead of individually is to keep them in their relative position. Notice that when Hickory Dog is squashed, his arms are still stuck to his shoulders, his tail is still in place, and so forth. If you'd done each piece individually, each one would have a slightly different amount of squash and stretch, which is okay; but then you'd have to realign them—not okay. Doing that makes it obvious that Hickory is just a bunch of chunks.

Now the rock should bounce off of Hickory's head. Lots of things could happen from there, but because this is a squash and stretch exercise, we'll make Hickory resume his original shape.

1. Add a keyframe for the rock at frame 10. Use the provided motion path as shown in Figure 4.30, or draw your own to make the rock bounce off Hickory and hit the ground. Set a tween with easing at –80 and rotate clockwise (CW) once.

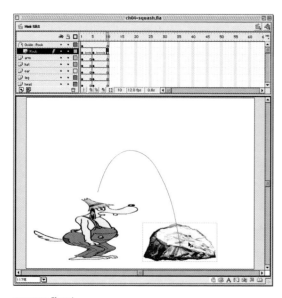

Figure 4.30 Floop!

2. Copy the Hickory Dog keyframes at frame 1 and paste them into frame 10. Set a tween for all the Hickory Dog layers between frames 5 and 10, with easing at –100.

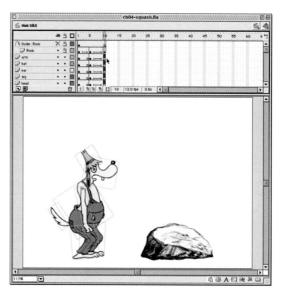

Figure 4.31 Copy-n-paste keyframes.

Play it and watch Hickory snap back into shape. If it doesn't happen fast enough to be funny, move the row of Hickory Dog keyframes over to frame 9 or 8, or adjust the easing. Scrub through the animation, and notice that Hickory's parts stay in their relative positions throughout the tween. In the key pose at frame 5, you can rotate Hickory's arms and tail to give him more of a reaction to being hit by a rock, as shown in Figure 4.32. His parts still appear to be connected to his body.

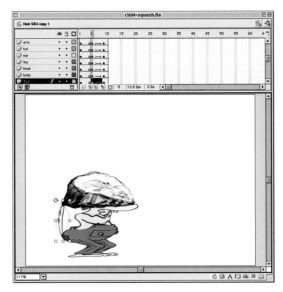

Figure 4.32 When the rock hits, Hickory's tail flies up.

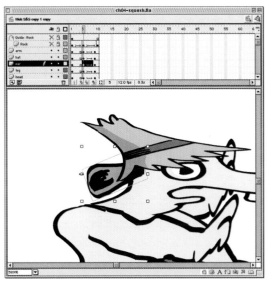

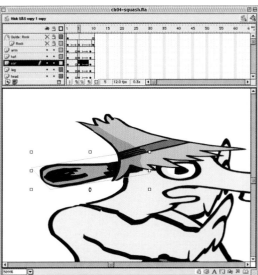

Figure 4.33 If necessary, rotate the piece, do the squash and stretch, and then rotate back into place.

One thing to note here is that although Hickory should maintain his volume throughout this bit of squash and stretch, not all of his parts need to squash and stretch the same amount. For example, his ears should probably stretch out and go long instead of short and fat. The same could go for his arms. But that's all for you to decide. Make it nice! The important thing is to try and keep all the pieces together as though they were connected where the joints really would be on a mutant dog. That way, your tweens will always look good with minimal fixes afterward.

Suppose you need to squash and stretch something that's at an angle, like Hickory Dog's ear as shown in Figure 4.33. If you try to squash and/or stretch it, it will scale at that rotation, giving it a skew where you may not want it. To avoid this, rotate the piece until it's completely horizontal or vertical; then do your squash and stretch on it, and rotate it back into place. It's a little extra work, but it makes a difference on certain types of parts—especially arms and heads, which look odd if distorted improperly.

TIMING

Animation without time is a series of drawings, just like a movie without time is a series of photos. A good sense of timing is absolutely critical to character animation. A change in timing can change the meaning of a scene. Sometimes one frame makes the difference between funny and boring. One of the most useful tools for an animator (besides observation and a mirror) is a stopwatch. If you're going to animate a bouncing ball, drop a ball and time it. If you're going to animate a character jumping, jump in the air and time it. Knowing how long actions really take will help you figure out how many frames those actions should take in your animation.

> **TIP** More frames between poses means slower actions. Fewer frames between poses means faster actions.

Generally speaking, fast is funny. It's not always true that fast is funny, but it usually is. Even if you're not trying to be funny, remember this: When in doubt, use fewer frames, especially when you're doing your next flying text job. Haven't we all suffered enough through text crawling across the screen? Give your actions just enough time to register, and move on. Keep 'em snappy. If the audience doesn't "get" the action, it's usually because the key poses aren't strong enough, not because it goes by too fast. In a world where cable TV channels number in the hundreds, people have learned to grasp images quickly. Producers lay down those rapid-fire sequences as standard practice; the editing techniques born of 30-second commercials and music videos have transformed our ability to accept visual input.

This is by no means suggesting that you should never have a slow moment in your animation. A slow scene might be a brilliant example of introspective character animation with great emotional depth. But more often than not it's just plain old boring. Usually it's because the animator didn't have enough business for the characters to do.

Slow moments do, in fact, have an important role: punctuation. If you've got a pause before a funny moment, that funny moment should go fast. It's the juxtaposition that makes it funny. Slow and slow is (usually) not funny. Fast and fast is (usually) funny but can get tiresome. Slow and fast, or fast and slow—now you're talkin'.

There's no real formula for timing. It's trial and error, and, above all, feel. It's far more important for your animation to *feel* right than to be technically accurate. Remember, animation is exaggeration. If you're going to exaggerate the real world, you have to know what to exaggerate, and how much. And you can't know that until you carefully observe the real-world equivalent of a specific action. We're not suggesting that you should drop a rock on your head, or anyone else's (kids—don't try this at home). But you can drop a rock. And you can act out what it would be like to have a heavy object fall on your head. How long after the rock falls until it hits? How long after the rock hits until it lands on the ground? How long after the rock hits until the character reacts? That's timing.

If the issue of timing is still making you scratch your head, steal (but always steal from the best!). Watch classic cartoons—frame by frame, if you can—and see what their timing is like. You may feel like you're just rehashing clichés, but there's a reason why they're time-honored clichés: they always work.

Besides, they're not clichés at all—they're the language of cartoons. Better you should speak the language of the classics than try to make up your own that few people understand. Look for a situation that's similar to one you want to use, and watch how they time their actions. How long does Wile E. Coyote hang in the air before he realizes he's stepped off a cliff? How long between blinks? How long do the eyes stay closed? How long after he realizes he's stepped off a cliff before he falls?

"When I put down a twelve-frame hold, that didn't mean thirteen frames or eleven frames, it meant twelve frames exactly. When the Coyote fell off, I knew he had to go exactly eighteen frames into the distance and then disappear for fourteen frames before he hit. A new animator would come in and he would overlap that, and it would never work."

—Chuck Jones (from *A Flurry of Drawings* by Hugh Kenner, University of California Press)

So how do you figure out your timing? Test, test, test your movie. Playing your movie within Flash is okay, but it's not the same thing as playing it back in the Flash player. When you test your movie, adjust the window so the movie plays at the right size. Remember that the bigger the movie, the slower it goes. Launch an .swf in the Flash player, or a browser window. Now change the size and see how it affects playback (and, therefore, the timing). Only by playing back your movie at the target size will you know if your timing feels right.

There are other factors to take into account. Changing the frame rate changes the timing. You can never be sure of what kind of computer your viewers are using, and computer power affects timing, too. Moving many things at once can be processor intensive, and will slow the animation, so you may need to compensate by taking out some frames. Certain kinds of effects, like Alpha tweens, are extremely processor intensive, so bear in mind the affect this will have on your character's timing.

STRAIGHT AHEAD AND POSE-TO-POSE

Pose-to-pose is like playing a melody, while straight-ahead is like doing a guitar solo. There are pros and cons to each method. While they are both perfectly valid methods of animation, you should probably lean more towards pose-to-pose with Flash because you're most likely going to be making short animations, where every second counts. If you were doing a feature-length animation, you'd have more screen time, and you could animate straight-ahead and see where that takes you. But it's a good idea to learn how to play your guitar before you start trying to solo.

You can do a combination of pose-to-pose and straight-ahead, if you're feeling confident. If you know exactly what the intent of your scene is (such as why this scene is in your animation), you know your characters well, and you storyboarded carefully, set just a few key poses and see what happens. It might lead to something funny. But then again, you might end up redoing the scene several times. See? Animation isn't for wimps.

Here's how to do pose-to-pose animation: Start with the idea. What's going to happen to whom in this scene? How about good ol' Hickory Dog trying to catch a chicken! The action will go like this: Hickory will stand in front of the chicken, rear back, lunge forward to grab the chicken, and smack the rock the chicken was standing on. Crack open the file called pose2pose.fla from the CD-ROM, select the pose2pose exercise scene, and follow these steps:

1. The first key pose is at frame 1, and it clearly establishes the situation. Hickory Dog spots the chicken but the chicken doesn't spot him, as shown in Figure 4.34.
2. Add a row of keyframes for all of Hickory's parts at frame 5. This is a wild guess for timing—you'll adjust it later. Select all of Hickory Dog except his legs and then rotate him back, as shown in Figure 4.35.

0

Figure 4.34 Oooh, a chicken!

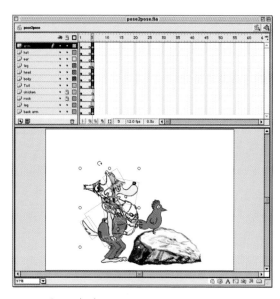

Figure 4.35 Rotate the dawg.

3. Now move the rotated Hickory chunks back onto his legs (Figure 4.36).

4. Pose Hickory's arms, head, ears, and whatnot to make him really lean back and anticipate lunging for the chicken, as shown in Figure 4.37. Be extreme! If a symbol is hidden behind other parts, clicking on the layer will select the symbol.

5. Now set another row of keyframes at frame 8, and pose Hickory Dog lunging for the chicken. Use a little squash and stretch to emphasize it. Figure 4.38 shows Hickory in a rather contorted state.

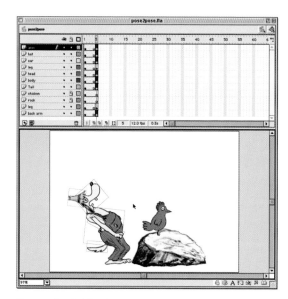

Figure 4.36 Now he's leaning.

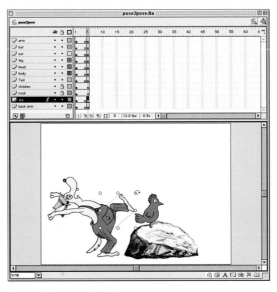

Figure 4.37 I'm gunna git you!

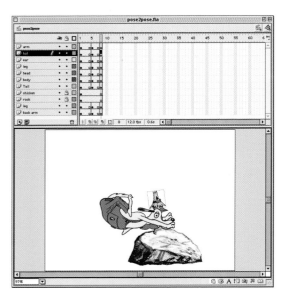

Figure 4.38 That's some lunge you got there.

We've got three poses so far, with anticipation and action. Now we need a reaction. Should Hickory catch the chicken? Of course not! While adjusting Hickory's hat, it somehow ended up on the chicken's head, and that seemed like a funny image. So let's make the chicken escape with Hickory's hat, as shown in Figure 4.39.

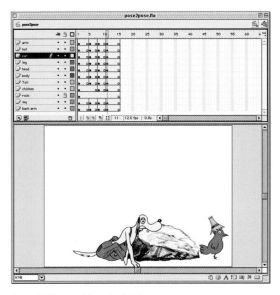

Figure 4.39 Dang, and he got m'hat, too.

Add a row of keyframes, including one for the chicken, at frame 11. Move the chicken and the hat together and the pose Hickory in a suitably pathetic position. Remember to remove the squash and stretch. You might find it easier to copy the keyframes from frame 1 and pose from there. Add some blank frames after the last keyframes.

When you play this back, you should be able to "read" the action. Set your key poses without any tweening—if the action plays well and is clear, it'll only get better with tweening. But tweening before that makes it harder to get a sense of the timing. Cartoon actions must always be clear. Keep them simple and precise. Being funny is a serious business.

Loopy

Always have Loop Playback on (Control > Loop Playback). There's no way to get a feel for your animation without watching it over and over again. What might seem perfectly fine the first time may, with repeated viewing, become unacceptable. Maybe there's a bit of arm movement that isn't right, or a blink that's in the wrong place, or a leg that slips off its joint for a frame. Animation is not for people who can't stand repetition. If you're watching something over and over again and it's still funny to you, it'll probably be funny to other people.

The key poses were set at arbitrary frames—another luxury you have that traditional animators don't. Now you need to adjust the timing to make the action as clear as possible. Watch it several times. Does it work as is?

No, it doesn't. There are a couple of things wrong with it: The anticipation is too quick, the lunge is too slow, and the pose where Hickory smacks the rock is wrong. He needs to really hit the rock—right now, he just hovers over it. If you're having trouble seeing it, add tweens temporarily and watch the animation. The timing should be clear just from the key poses. When you get used to working this way, you'll learn how to watch key poses and see timing problems. This will be useful in the animatic stage. For clarity, the keyframes will be labeled Start, Lean, Lunge, and Lump. (All of this has been done in the pose2pose copy 1 scene in the pose2pose.fla.)

Add some frames between Start and Lean. This is the anticipation of the action, and it needs to slow down a bit. Add one frame at a time and then play it back. Keep adding frames until it looks right. Three frames are about right, so keyframe Lean is at frame 8.

The lunge is too slow, so take out some frames between Lean and Lunge. Again, take out one frame at a time and then play it until it looks right. It's not necessarily a bad thing to have no frames between keyframes. Remember that if your frame rate is 12 fps, you're effectively animating "on twos" for every one frame. In this case, take out one frame so keyframe Lunge is at frame 10.

Now adjust the Lunge pose so Hickory whacks the rock with full force. Leave the chicken and the hat where they are. The following steps should yield a magnificent belly flop:

1. Select all of Hickory Dog's parts, and move him down to contact the rock, as shown in Figure 4.40.

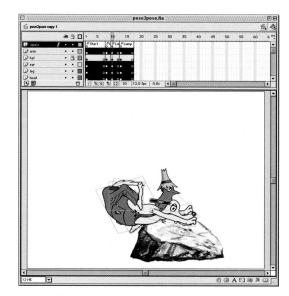

Figure 4.40 We have contact.

2. Rotate and move Hickory's body, legs, and tail so they're way up in the air. Once again, exaggerate! Figure 4.41 should give you a good idea of where to go with this.

3. Tip his head back, and use his arm to cover up the seam between the head and the body (Figure 4.42). Cheat wherever necessary (or possible) to get the effect you want.

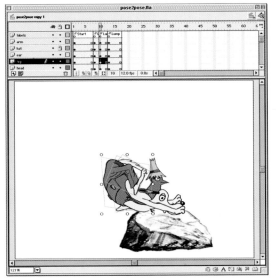

Figure 4.41
Flying mutant dog yoga.

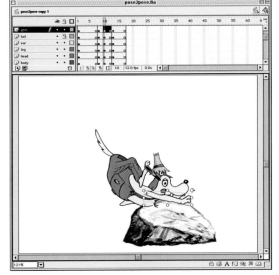

Figure 4.42
Adjust the tail and legs to get a good clear line of action.

Now there's a new problem, one that violates one of the cardinal rules of animation: One Action at a Time. In the present scenario, Hickory lunges for the chicken and then the chicken escapes as Hickory falls down. Which will draw the audience's eyes? It's hard to say, and that means the action will be unclear. Fixing this might actually make it funnier, too. If Hickory Dog lunges for a chicken, misses, and lands on his butt, that seems like a reasonable thing to happen. But if Hickory Dog lunges for a chicken, misses, hangs in the air while the chicken saunters off screen, stays in the air long enough to be funny, and *then* falls, now you're talking good old-fashioned cartoon values. You can keep the same key poses—just fiddle with the timing:

1. Add some frames between Lunge and Lump, so Lump is now at frame 20 (Figure 4.43).

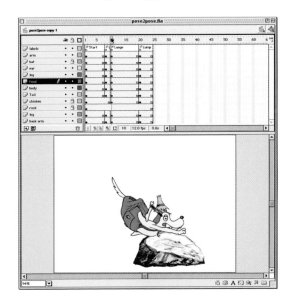

Figure 4.43 Lunge time!

2. Move the keyframes for the chicken and the hat somewhere in between Lunge and Lump. Label it Chicken (Figure 4.44).

3. Get the chicken off screen, as in Figure 4.45, so Hickory can fall (one action at a time). Add keyframes for the chicken and the hat around frame 16 and then move them off screen.

4. Put a blank keyframe (F7) after the chicken and the hat's last keyframes to make them disappear, as shown in Figure 4.46. This will make it more clear to you what's happening on screen, and give Flash less to work on. Adjust the timing of when Hickory falls by adding or subtracting frames before Lump to make it funnier.

If you're satisfied with the timing so far, add tweens for all the keyframes, and see what you've got. Clearly, there's a lot more work to be done on this one to make it nice. But the timing is about right, and the action is clear because the key poses worked first. That's pose-to-pose with a little straight-ahead improv with the hat on the chicken.

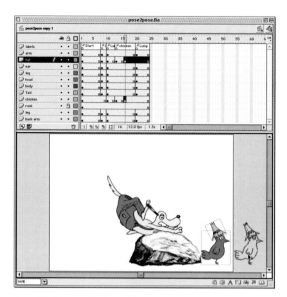

Figure 4.45 Chicken exits, stage right.

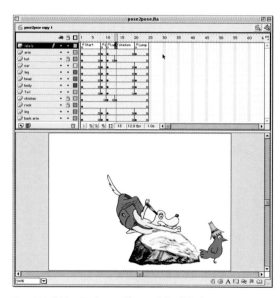

Figure 4.44 Chicken Keyframes. It's a specialty of the house.

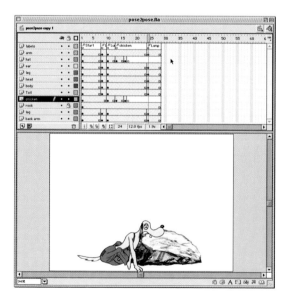

Figure 4.46 Where'd he go?

EXAGGERATION

Animation is exaggeration. By exaggeration, we mean distilling the essence of an action or character and then emphasizing it. All due respect to Ralph Bakshi, nothing is more boring than rotoscoped animation (live action traced frame-for-frame). It's a copy of real life, the cartoon equivalent of photo-realism. There's no artistic interpretation involved.

What makes animation interesting and watchable is the animator's "take," or point of view. This is in the character design, key poses, and timing. The entire animation should reflect a point of view—the more specific and unique the take on things, the better. Much of what establishes that point of view is the choice of what to exaggerate. Animation isn't inherently about exaggeration, but good animation is.

When posing your characters, always push the extremes. A key pose can look bizarre and unrealistic, but if it captures an action, it works. Also, you'll be seeing that pose for a single frame (unless it's a held pose), and then it will tween into something else. Exaggerating your key poses gives your animation snap and vitality. You'll find that the most unrealistic poses can lead to the most convincing animation.

There's no such thing as "too extreme" in animation. You can certainly exaggerate the wrong things, or the right things at the wrong time, but you can't exaggerate too much. Think of the crazed histrionics of Ren and Stimpy.

In the previous example of Hickory Dog trying to catch the chicken, Hickory had four key poses. The first key pose didn't require much exaggeration. But the second, when he leaned back in anticipation of the lunging action, could look like Figure 4.47.

Figure 4.47 A sneaky Hickory Dog.

Or it could look like this Figure 4.48.

Figure 4.48 A good breeze would knock him over.

Or you could push it even further with some squash and stretch, or a new drawing. Which version captures the action of Hickory rearing back to lunge for the chicken? Which one "sells" it best?

Exaggeration is not always about making funny key poses. Even the most subtle moments of acting require careful exaggeration. Movie actors primarily use their faces—the eyes in particular—to convey emotion. Cartoon actors use their entire bodies to convey emotion. If you can read a character's emotions through its pose and gesture, you'll have a strong scene. After that, any facial animation is just icing on the cake. But if you rely entirely on facial animation or dialogue to get your point across, it's likely to be missed.

The two silhouetted poses of Ford shown in Figure 4.49 use the exact same pieces (with the exception of the back arm). Can you guess how he might be feeling in each one? Take a look at scene 1 in the fordPoses.fla file on the CD-ROM to see the individual pieces.

Figure 4.49 The power of the puppet.

Cartoon acting is always very broad and theatrical. It doesn't need to be realistic—it needs to be convincing.

ANTICIPATION

Anticipation is the action before the action. It's an action in the opposite direction of the main action to follow. When Hickory Dog lunges for the chicken, he doesn't go from a total standstill

to being on top of the rock. He leans back, getting ready to lunge forward. There's two reasons why he does this. He needs to gather momentum to lunge at the chicken. Hickory's not very strong. Also, it draws the audience's eye to the action. The eye is naturally drawn to things that move. Anticipation tells the audience where to look.

Remember, tell your audience what you're going to do, do it, then tell them you did it: Anticipation, action, reaction. Without anticipation, your characters' actions will seem to come out of nowhere, and may happen before the audience knows who or what to look at.

Establish anticipation with key poses. Act out the action, and see where you naturally anticipate. If your character is going to stand up from a chair, sit in a chair and then stand up. You'll most likely lean forward, put your hands on the arms or your knees, and then stand up. Standing up is the main action. Leaning forward is the anticipation. So you'll need a key pose for the character sitting, a key pose for the character standing, and between those, a key pose of the character leaning over. Here's Ford sitting (Figure 4.50) and standing (Figure 4.51). He needs an anticipatory lean between these two poses.

Figure 4.50 Whattya sitting around for?   Figure 4.51 I'm up, I'm up!

When you open the file, Ford should be sitting on a blue box, as shown in Figure 4.52:

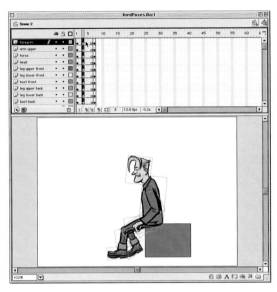

Figure 4.52 Ford, sitting.

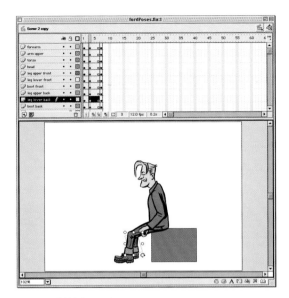

Figure 4.53 Get his leg ready.

1. Ford moves his feet back a bit and then stand, so copy the keyframe of the back boot to the keyframe at frame 3, and adjust the rest of the leg to match the foot, as shown in Figure 4.53. The same goes for the front leg. This keeps his feet planted while he stands up.
2. Select all of Ford's upper body parts and then rotate them forward, as shown in Figure 4.54.

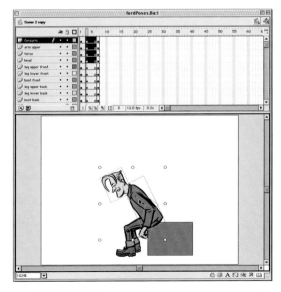

Figure 4.54 Rotate his torso.

3. Adjust Ford's front arm to put his hand on his knee. Rotate the upper arm, and then move the forearm to keep the shoulder in place. We'll cheat the back arm so it isn't seen (Figure 4.55).

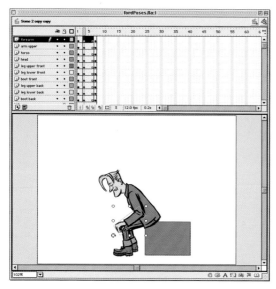

Figure 4.55 Cheating is allowed. Encouraged, even.

Add tweens for the keyframes and then see what it looks like. It needs tweaking; the knees shift, he should plant his arms on his knees first and then start standing up, and the timing is off. But he's anticipating the action now.

To make it nice, you'll need to adjust Ford's pose in a couple of places. As you can see, letting Flash tween him into place just isn't cutting the mustard. In this case, Ford needs to keep his feet locked to the ground, so don't set any extra keyframes for the feet. That also means his ankles have to appear to be attached to his feet. Adjust the body by selecting the torso, head, and arms and rotating them all at once. This keeps the arm and head locked in place; then move this upper body group according to where the hips should go.

Watch those joints! You don't want them sliding all over the place. This is an admittedly counter-intuitive way to work, but it's really the only way. Flash has no tools for keeping the joints together, so you have to do it manually.

Now adjust the legs to match the torso where the hips would be. Start from the lower legs and work your way up. Move the lower leg according to where the knee needs to be, and rotate it back to match the ankle position. Move the upper leg according to where the hip should be and then rotate it to meet the lower leg.

The same goes for the arm. The hand has to stay on the knee. The upper arm only rotates, not moves, so adjust the forearm first and then make the upper arm match. All you can do is guess about where the elbow should go; then rotate it until the hand is on the knee where it should be (according to the previous key pose). If it isn't, move it, rotate it, and see if you can rotate the upper arm to meet the forearm at the elbow. Keep trying—it can be done! Animation isn't for sissies!

There's a little opportunity to cheat here: You can use the hand to cover up any problems you might have keeping the knee in place. It's best, however, to get it right, which you can check by temporarily hiding the arm and any other layers that might cover the joint you're adjusting. Otherwise, the pose will feel "loose" and any other poses that have the joints in slightly different positions won't match, making his actions inconsistent at best, and spastic at worst.

Overshoot

Overshoot is a type of anticipation. Instead of anticipating the main action, overshoot anticipates the end pose. It's the action after the action. It goes beyond the end pose, and then eases into it, making actions snappier and more convincing.

After Ford stands up, reaching his final key pose, he stops. With overshoot, he would stand up a little straighter and then settle into his slight slouch. You can add these steps to your Scene 2 exercise scene, or just take a look at the overshoot copy and overshoot scenes:

1. Add a row of keyframes at frame 11 (except for the boots). This will duplicate the last key pose (Figure 4.56). These are the keyframes that Ford will settle into.

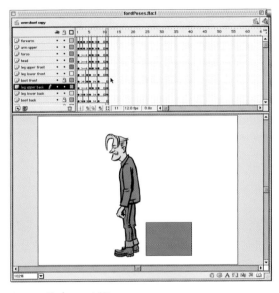

Figure 4.56 Keyframes at 11!

2. Go to the original end key pose at frame 8 and stand Ford up a little straighter. Make sure he's a bit taller, his body leans back, his arms straighten out (Figure 4.57), and his head tips back. Adjusting the legs takes extra effort, but it's worth it.

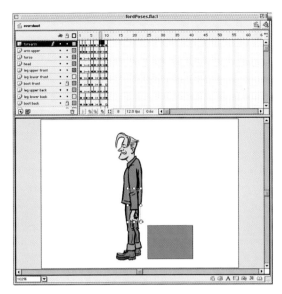

Figure 4.57 Add a little starch.

Now add tweens between the overshoot key pose and the end key pose. Make sure it eases out a bit (40 is about right).

This works for the end of almost any action, and makes it feel more natural. Set your end key pose and then add another set of keyframes after it. Go back to the original end key pose and make it more extreme, add tweening and adjust the number of frames between them until it feels right. Sometimes you don't need any frames between the keyframes, which is fine for faster actions. Your character will settle into the end pose instead of immediately coming to a dead stop (although that can be funny sometimes). This works great in combination with squash and stretch.

You can use overshoot to spice up a boring flying text job. Suppose you've got some text to enlarge, like the word Twinkle in flyingtext.fla. First of all, stifle the urge to make this go slowly. Ten frames is way too long, and no easing!?! Unacceptable! In the name of all things jolly, make it nice!

Five frames of this will be plenty. Ease in or out? That's up to you. Now add an extra keyframe after the last one. Go back to the original end keyframe, and scale it up a bit, as shown in Figure 4.58. See? A single keyframe can save this from being a snorefest. If you want, add a frame and some easing between the last two keyframes, but you're probably best off keeping it snappy. Even if it's dull corporate work, it's still animation.

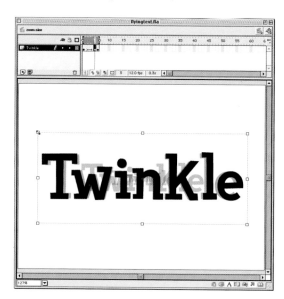

Figure 4.58 Add just a little more sproink!

Bouncing

Pound your fist on a stable surface, like a table. When your fist hits, it's going to bounce back up a bit and then come to rest on the table. How much depends on how hard you hit the table, and how sturdy the table is. This is a type of overshoot, except your fist can't go through the table to overshoot the stopping point, so instead it bounces back. Nearly everything bounces, even if it's just a little bit. Properly applied, bouncing can really give your chunks a feeling of weight. Crack open the file bounce.fla and play the okay scene of Ford's arm as he puts down his beverage. It's just okay, as the scene name implies. Nothing special.

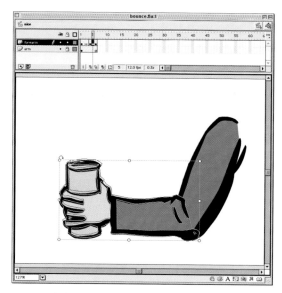

Figure 4.59 Clank!

Add two keyframes after the last Forearm keyframe. Add two frames of Arm, so the Arm doesn't just disappear. Now go to the keyframe at frame 5, which is between two identical keyframes. Rotate the forearm clockwise slightly to make it bounce. That's all there is to it. The results can be seen in the nice scene, as shown in Figure 4.59. If you want, you can adjust the keyframe either before or after the bounce keyframe. You can also make your chunks bounce several times—just add two more keyframes for each extra bounce. Again, this can be combined with a little squash and stretch.

FOLLOW-THROUGH AND OVERLAPPING ACTION

What these two principles boil down to is this: Not everything stops at once. The exact difference between the two is difficult to distinguish and not very important. What's important is to realize that when something comes to a stop, the various parts stop at different times. Most of this is due to momentum. *The Illusion of Life* lists five categories of follow-through and overlap, but you'll mostly only deal with three: appendages, completion, and moving hold. The other two, jelly bellies and chubby cheeks, are a little harder to manage without resorting to cel-style animation.

Appendages

Appendages such as arms, long floppy ears, tails, and so forth keep going after the bulk of the character they belong to stops moving. How much depends on how fast the character is moving before the stop, and how much the parts weigh. The heavier the part, the sooner it stops. For example, if Hickory Dog were walking and then stopped, his feet would stop first, then his arms, then his tail, then his ears. Now it's true that he often doesn't move his arms when he walks because he's so stupid, but you get the idea.

You probably don't have a tail or long floppy ears, but try walking and then coming to a stop. Your arms will continue their swing after your feet have stopped—the forward foot first, and then the back foot. It seems obvious, but it's worth mentioning that your arms will continue the swing in progress and then come to a rest. They probably don't change direction or swing wildly out of control. The lesson to be learned is that follow-through and overlap should be a natural progression of the action in progress as it comes to a stop.

In the previous example of Ford standing up, there's a column of keyframes at frames 8 and 11 (Figure 4.60). That means that all of Ford's parts stop at the same time. Depending on how Ford feels, it's okay for his legs, torso, and even his head to stop at the same time, but the arms definitely have to keep moving. In a perfect world, adding some follow-through and overlap would be as simple as moving the arm keyframes over a few frames and letting the tweening do the work.

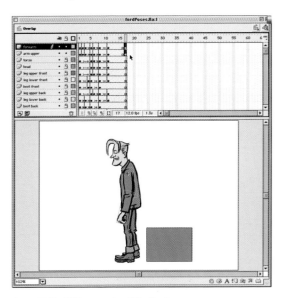

Figure 4.60 Stop! Take a gander at the Overlap scene.

But that would be too easy. If you do that, Ford's arms will come apart at the joints for a few frames and then float back into place. Try it and see for yourself. You want to keep the arm locked to the shoulder on the torso, and the forearm locked to the elbow during the swing. And that takes keyframes. You'll still have columns of keyframes to keep the joints in place, but you'll add keyframes before or after the columns and manually adjust them to add follow-through and overlap. For this example, we'll only deal with Ford's arms. His final pose will be the same as the one currently in the animation, but his body will stop first. His arms will swing forward and then settle into the final pose a few frames later.

1. Add some extra frames after the last keyframe. Add keyframes for the upper arm and forearm symbols at the last frame. This is the end pose.

2. Go back to the column of keyframes at frame 11 and adjust the arm to swing further out than the current rest position. Rotate the upper arm first move the forearm to meet it at the elbow, and rotate the forearm, as shown in Figure 4.61. The arm should have some pretty good momentum.

3. Set keyframes for both arm pieces somewhere between the body's end pose and the last frame. Now pose the arm to the fullest extent of the swing, as shown in Figure 4.62.

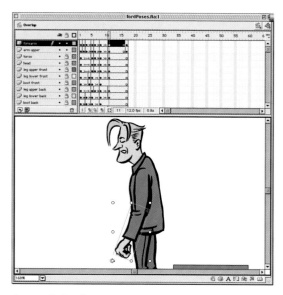

Figure 4.61 Capture the momentum.

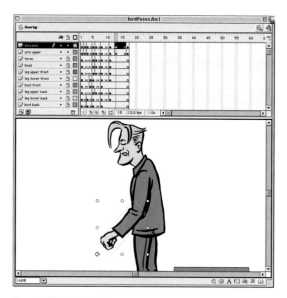

Figure 4.62 The arm posed.

4. Add tweens and check your timing. The tween should ease out for both parts of the swing. If the swing feels too extreme, adjust the pose or the number of frames. Figure 4.63 shows the swinging arm in onion skin.

Figure 4.63
The swinging arm.

If you really want to make it nice, do a little "successive breaking of joints" and have the upper arm stop first, and then the forearm. It's overlapping the overlap. Also, the elbow should be at its most bent just after the full extent of the swing.

1. Add a forearm keyframe just after the mid-swing keyframe. Rotate the forearm at the new keyframe to be as bent as it was on the previous keyframe. Adjust the previous keyframe to be slightly less bent (Figure 4.64).

2. Add some extra frames after the end keyframes. Add a forearm keyframe after the current end forearm keyframe. Rotate the old forearm end keyframe to be slightly more bent (Figure 4.65).

Figure 4.64 A slight tweak—as shown in the SBJ scene.

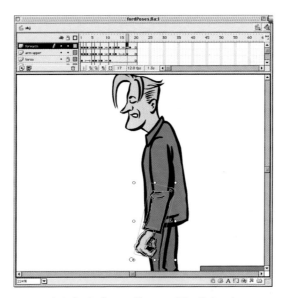

Figure 4.65 Just a few keyframes with some subtle adjustments can make a big difference.

You may find that the timing needs adjustment. If you want to go hog wild, you can make the arm swing past the end pose slightly and then come to rest because the action still feels a little abrupt. Also, you can make the torso straighten out after the legs stop, and maybe do a little overlap with the head. Make it nice!

Completion

After you've got the concept of follow-through and overlap down, the next question to tackle is: How does the character follow through? The way the character completes the action can say more than the action itself. It can be a gag: The action is the setup, and the follow-through is the payoff. The classic example is the baseball player who swings the bat so hard that he twists himself into a spiral.

In the previous example, the action was Ford standing up, which isn't too revealing of his character. The follow-through was his arms swinging as he settled into his slouch. But he could have stood up and flailed off-balance for an instant (Figure 4.66). Or he could have stood up, and immediately flopped over (Figure 4.67). The possibilities are endless, as long as they're in character. Ford might have stood up, and immediately snapped to attention and saluted, but it's not too likely for the kind of guy he is. But one too many Hi-Boy beers, and you get Figure 4.66 or 4.67 (see the completion scene in fordPoses.fla).

Figure 4.66 All that's missing is the banana peel.

Figure 4.67 Call a chiropractor!

Moving Hold

Movement equals life in animation, so keep your characters moving. This does not mean your characters should flail constantly. Every action should be clear and precise—otherwise, you're just moving stuff around on the screen. What it does mean is after the anticipation, the action, the overshoot, the follow-through and overlap—when your character has stopped moving—the character keeps on moving.

People move constantly, unless they're dead or cryogenically frozen. Even when they're trying to be still, they breathe, blink, or stir a little bit. Try not moving and see how much effort it takes. It's no use trying to study yourself at rest, because you'll be too conscious of what you're doing. Watch other people just standing around or sitting, and note the kinds of things they do. They shift their weight, tap their feet, fold and unfold their arms, look around and try to avoid the creep staring at them, things like that. It doesn't have to be a whole lot of movement, and probably shouldn't. Sometimes just a look or a blink is enough. Or set a slightly different key pose and tween back and forth between the two.

Watch the Other Characters

One test of how well something is animated is to watch the characters that aren't the focus of the scene (usually this means the one who isn't talking). Check out Princess Dot and the other little ants in *A Bug's Life* when her class unveils the painting of the "warriors" to see what we mean. If two characters are having a conversation, what's the other one doing? Are they staying in character? This sort of attention to detail makes the classics endlessly watchable.

SECONDARY ACTION

Anticipation is the action before the action. Follow-through and overlap are the actions after the action. Secondary action is the action *during* the action. It's the little things that happen while the big thing is happening. The chunks on which you would do a little follow-through and overlap are the same ones that get the secondary actions: arms, floppy ears, tails, clothes, and so on. Facial expressions can be considered secondary actions as well.

Secondary actions should add to the main action, not distract from it. Otherwise, the secondary action becomes a primary action itself, and then you have two things happening at once, violating the cardinal rule: One action at a time.

Secondary actions should be dealt with in the same manner as follow-through and overlap. Set key poses and animate the main action first, so it's clear what's going on; then add keyframes around the keyframe columns to keep the joints in place, and adjust the individual parts. The main action will suggest secondary actions.

IN CONCLUSION...

Paper cutouts have nothing on Flash. In the next chapter, you'll apply what you've learned to the most challenging aspect of character animation: the walk cycle.

5

Character Chunks and Walk Cycles

This chapter will show you how to cut apart and reassemble your characters to get the most out of your drawings. You'll start out by learning how to deal with those pesky elbow and knee joints as you work up to the all-important walk cycle. Along the way, you'll learn about shape tweens, looping, and facial animation.

WORKING WITH JOINTS

Elbows and knees are some of the most difficult body chunks to work with in Flash. If an elbow slips out of place for a single frame, it's noticeable and, therefore, unacceptable. The goal is to maintain the illusion of a continuous line drawing, even though the limbs are really just moving chunks. Because Flash lacks the tools necessary to keep joints together, a lot of your orthopedic work comes down to brute force keyframing. In theory, you could keep the limb chunks together through nested symbols, such as an arm symbol containing the upper and lower arm. In practice, however, it's extremely difficult to work with digital puppets built with a nested symbol methodology; nested symbol limbs are hard to change, and easy to screw up.

Knowing how to cut elbows and knees apart, what to fill in, and where to put the center point is critical to making a successful digital puppet—at least, a digital puppet that can be easily posed.

Figure 5.1
Hey, what
happened
to his arm?

Much of this is tied into the art itself, but there are some general guidelines. Take the drawing of Ford, shown in Figure 5.1—it's the original Doug Allen drawing upon which the Ford walk cycle was based.

Knees

Cut them off at (well, maybe just a hair below) the knees! Look closely at the knees in Figure 5.2. Both have some cloth folds at the back of the knees, which is helpful. But the knee on the left has a line for the kneecap, while the knee on the right doesn't. The kneecap can cover up the shin joint. But the knee on the right is undefined, so to cut that apart you'll have to pick a spot where the knee would go, and be accurate about keeping the joints lined up. Small character design details, like kneecaps, can make cutting apart the joints much easier.

Figure 5.2
The right knee
lacks a kneecap.

The following steps demonstrate how to construct a working knee joint. Open up the fordjoint.fla file from the CD-ROM. Select the exercise scene:

1. Copy the lower part of the front leg including some of the knee. Create a new layer (front leg lower), paste the leg chunk in place, and hide the Original layer, as shown in Figure 5.3.

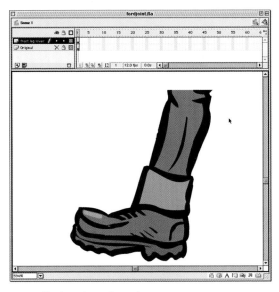

Figure 5.3 The lower leg on its own layer.

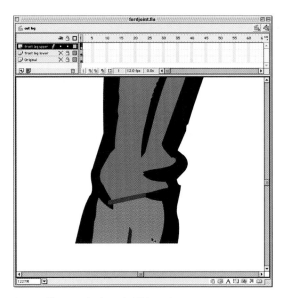

Figure 5.4 The upper leg layer should be on top.

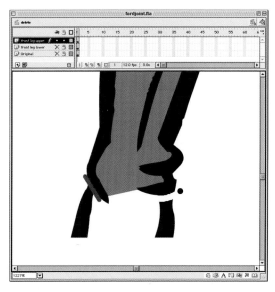

Figure 5.5 Trim carefully.

2. Copy the upper part of the front leg, including some of the shin. Create a new layer and then paste it in place (front leg upper), as shown in Figure 5.4. The upper leg should be above the lower leg in layer level. Both layers viewed together should look identical to the original (which you should lock off and hide).

3. The front leg is fully extended, so the lower leg will never rotate clockwise any further unless Ford breaks his leg. The kneecap and cloth folds will stay with the upper leg to cover up the lower leg joint. Lock off and hide the lower leg. Using the line tool, draw a temporary line between the kneecap and the tip of the bottom cloth fold, as shown in Figure 5.5. Use the Arrow tool to select the chunk of jeans below the line and delete it. Double-click on the line to select the line in its entirety, and delete it.

In this corner…Not every dog is a mutant hillbilly.

4. Use the Eraser tool or the temporary line technique to delete the calf lines below the knee (Figure 5.5). Use the Arrow tool to select the chunks and then delete them as well as any temporary lines. Adjust the kneecap and cloth fold lines as necessary. Lock the layer, and view it as outlines.

5. Draw a temp line well below the kneecap line, and delete out the blue chunk. Now use the Eraser tool or temp lines (Figure 5.6) to delete out the kneecap and cloth fold lines. It is important that the calf line (the one on the right) not be any longer than necessary, or it will limit how much you can bend Ford's leg. Reshape the lower leg lines if the curves need smoothing, but try to follow the original brushwork.

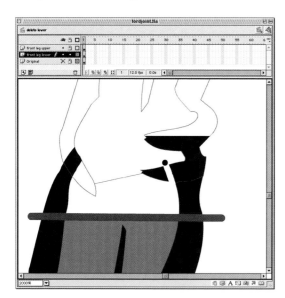

Figure 5.6 Cut 'em off just below the knee.

6. Draw a temp line between the tops of the two lines that make up the lower leg, and fill it with blue (Figure 5.7). Make sure the fill goes above the edge of the fill on the upper leg between the kneecap and cloth fold. Delete the temp line.

Figure 5.7 A smooth calf.

7. Group the lower leg, and make it a symbol. Edit the symbol, and move the leg so the center point is about where the kneecap line meets the leg line, as shown in Figure 5.8.

8. View the original and then move the lower leg back into place. To align the lower leg with the original them exactly, view both as outlines. Try rotating the leg, as shown in Figure 5.9. You may need to adjust the center point.

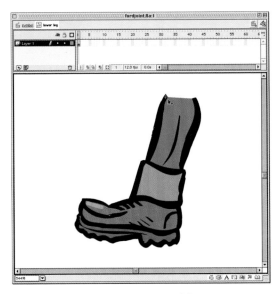

Figure 5.8 Set the leg symbol's centerpoint carefully.

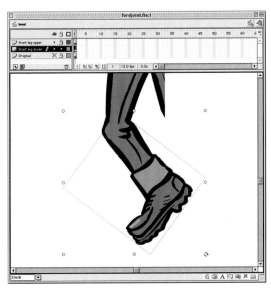

Figure 5.9 That leg ain't got a thing if it ain't got that swing.

Cutting apart the other knee works almost the same way, except there's no kneecap to cover up the joint. Follow the first step from the previous example. Place the back leg chunks on their own (respective) layers: back upper leg and back lower leg.

1. On the back upper leg layer, draw a temp line from the tip of the bottom cloth fold to where the knee should bend, as shown in Figure 5.10. Use the Arrow tool to select and then delete the unnecessary chunks. Erase or use a temp line to get rid of the calf line on the right. Delete the temp line(s).

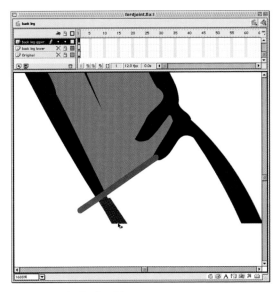

Figure 5.10 Get that line just right.

2. Using the Arrow tool, round out the flat side of the line you cut across at the knee, as shown in Figure 5.11. This helps smooth out the joint when the leg bends.

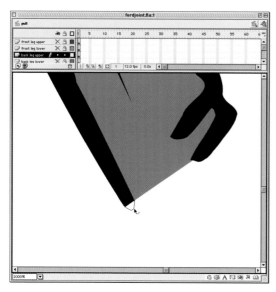

Figure 5.11 Round out the line.

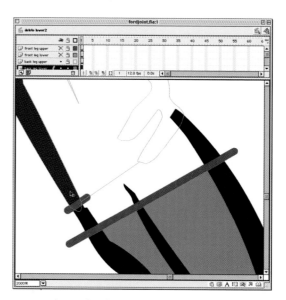

Figure 5.12 The temp line drawn.

3. On the back lower leg layer, draw a temp line well below the knee line (Figure 5.12) and delete out the blue chunk. Now use the Eraser tool or temp lines to delete out the cloth fold lines. Make sure the calf line continues into the cloth folds. Draw a temp line just above the knee cut on the upper leg, and delete the line above it.

4. Use the Arrow tool to round out the flat side of the line, as shown in Figure 5.13 (as you did in step 2). This rounded area is where the center point will be. Draw a temp line from the rounded tip to the extended calf line, and fill in the area with blue.

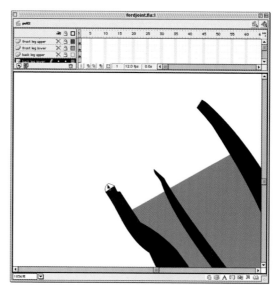

Figure 5.13 Round out this line, too.

5. Follow steps 6 and 7 above. If the blue edge of the upper leg chunk covers up the black line of the lower leg when it bends, pull the blue edge back away from the rounded tip, as shown in Figure 5.14.

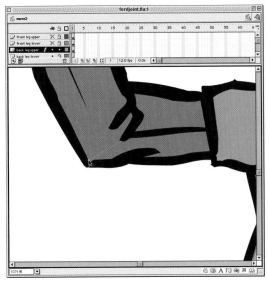

Figure 5.14 Look Mom, I'm an arthroscopic surgeon!

Elbows

Working with elbows is similar to working with knees. It's no accident that many characters are designed with long sleeves, or short sleeves that end right at the elbow. It's a cheat! If the character has long sleeves, then cutting out the elbow works exactly like the knees in the previous example. Keep the cloth folds with the forearm. If the character wears short sleeves that go up to the elbow, you can use a single forearm piece with the seam hidden by the sleeve. If the character has long sleeves or bare arms, the forearm will go in front of the upper arm.

Figure 5.15 shows Doug Allen's drawing of Jicketts' arm. The problem is making the arm capable of fully extending.

Figure 5.15 The original drawing.

Because the forearm is thinner than the upper arm, the upper arm will have to be longer to allow the arm to extend, as shown in Figure 5.16 but not so long as to keep the arm from bending.

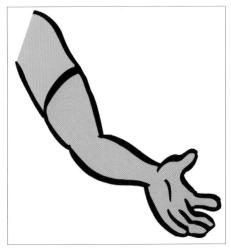

Figure 5.16
Fully extended.

As you can see in Figure 5.17, the arm cannot be bent up any further. You can cheat a little bit by moving the location of the elbow further up the arm as the arm extends down, but do this cautiously.

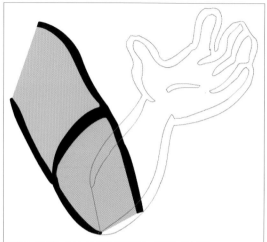

Figure 5.17
That's as far
as it goes.

One way around this problem, without resorting to making a new piece, is to mask off part of the arm in a new symbol. Open up the jickettsarm.fla file from the CD-ROM, and use the symbols in the library.

1. Make a new symbol. Place the upper arm symbol in it. Use the Info palette (Figure 5.18) to position the upper arm symbol's center at the center of the new symbol.

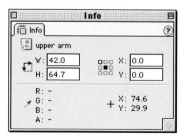

Figure 5.18
The Info palette allows
precise positioning.

2. Use a mask layer to mask off the bottom portion of the upper arm at an angle, as shown in Figure 5.19. Make sure not to mask off any of the elbow joint area.

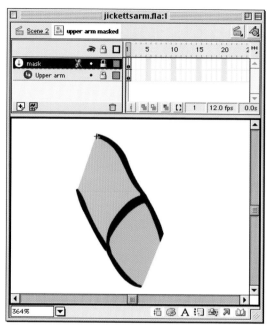

Figure 5.19
Set the mask.

3. To use this new symbol, just set a new keyframe in the upper arm layer. Then swap out the original upper arm symbol for the new, masked upper arm symbol, as shown in Figure 5.20.

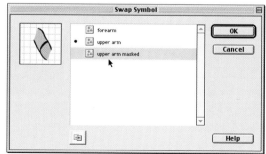

Figure 5.20
Swap symbol.

4. Now you can bend the forearm much further (Figure 5.21), depending on how much upper arm you masked off.

Figure 5.21
Amazing range
of motion!

PICKING UP CHUNKS

Little chunks can make all the difference. Suppose you have a single object that has parts that go in front of another object as well as behind the object, like the hand holding a can shown in Figure 5.22. As you can see, some fingers will go in front of the can, while others go behind the can. Clearly you can't use a single symbol for the hand if you intend to animate either one. Fortunately, this situation can be handled with ease. When you cut apart the front and back parts of the hand, make sure they both have the same center point. That way each piece will transform around the same center point and stay locked together.

Open up the frontandback.fla file from the CD-ROM, and select the exercise scene:

Figure 5.22
You got an I.D.
for that?

1. Make the hand chunk into a symbol. Adjust the center point as you would with any part. Copy the hand chunk, create a new layer, and paste it in place. In the top layer, delete out all the parts that do not need to go in front. You can leave the bottom layer as is, but it's a good idea to delete out the parts that go in front so as not to duplicate data (Figure 5.23).

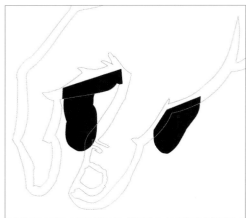

Figure 5.23
Be sure to leave some
overlap between
the chunks.

2. In the library controls, duplicate the symbol. Rename both symbols, one to indicate that it goes on top, the other to indicate it goes on the bottom, as shown in Figure 5.24. Edit the top one and delete the bottom piece layer. Edit the bottom one and delete the top piece layer.

Figure 5.24
Use descriptive names!

3. Place the piece with the most recognizable chunk in your scene. Copy its keyframe and paste it into a new layer (Figure 5.25).

4. Click on the symbol in the new layer and use swap symbol to change it to the other chunk. Make sure the layer with the chunk that goes in front is on top, and the layer with the chunk that goes behind is on the bottom. The chunk that goes between the two pieces gets sandwiched between their layers (Figure 5.26).

When you transform the top and bottom chunks, select them both and transform them together so they always match.

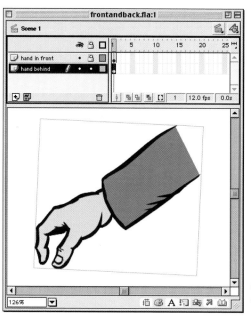

Figure 5.25
All you need now is that beer can.

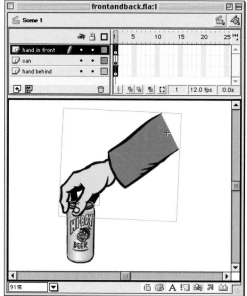

Figure 5.26
A top chunk, a bottom chunk, and a beer can in-between.

SHAPE TWEENS

Used sparingly, shape tweens can add flexibility to your animation that can't be achieved using chunks. The downside is that the pieces that are shape tweened have to be extremely simple, and for the most part, you'll end up keyframing and reshaping by hand. But just like motion tween, shape tween gets you most of the way there, and the rest is up to you.

Crack open the file shapetween.fla from the CD-ROM. As you can see in Figure 5.27, Hickory Dog is goofing off with his nose. There was really no way to do this animation without a shape tween on the nose, unless it was done like cel animation.

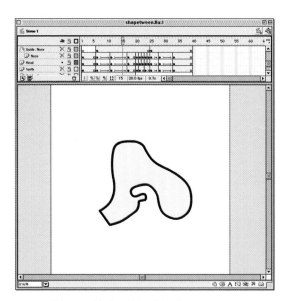

Figure 5.28 Take a good look at Hickory's head.

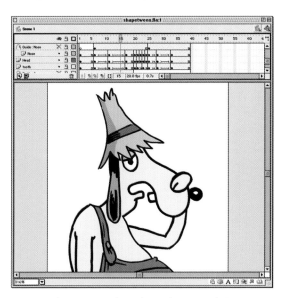

Figure 5.27 What's a mutant dog to do on a hot August day?

To see what's really going on, it helps to hide all the layers except the one labeled Head, as shown in Figure 5.28.

The initial position was drawn by tracing the original Doug Allen drawing using the Pencil tool. It was smoothed to limit the number of points on the curves. A line thickness was chosen to match the lines of the other chunks. The shape must be completely closed or Flash will get confused during the tween. Here the neck line is hidden by the body. Figure 5.29 shows Hickory's springy snout in action.

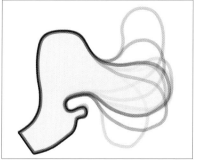

Figure 5.29
Twoing!

The key poses were set by reshaping the head chunk with the Arrow tool. When the nose springs up and down, each keyframe had to be adjusted by hand because the shape tween made a mess of the nose. Also, each pose had to have slightly less spring so it would appear to be slowing down. When there are isolated keyframes of the chunk, group it: because Flash deals with groups more efficiently. No shape hints were necessary in this case, but they can help if Flash can't figure out what to do on its own.

When using a shape tween piece this way, don't forget the secondary animation. You can use the extra parts (like the ear) to cover up any areas where the shape tween piece becomes misshapen.

FACIAL ANIMATION

Unless you know for a fact that the head won't be moving in a scene, do all your facial animation as scene-specific animated symbols. These can't be movie clips because they need to be tied to the main timeline and the sound. With the facial animation and lip sync nested in a symbol, you can then freely animate the head without worrying about the various parts floating around on the face.

Facial animation isn't nearly as important as body animation, so set your key poses first. Get the gestures and timing right so the story is told through actions. When the action is clear through just the key poses and tweening, add the final dialogue and then retime as necessary. Once you know the length of the scene and where the dialogue occurs, do the facial animation before you set too many head keyframes. (More on this later.)

Build the animated symbol of the head the way you would any other scene. There will be a head background—a head with no features except those that will not move, such as nose or ears.

Each piece that needs to move must have its own layer, preferably clearly labeled, as shown in Figure 5.30.

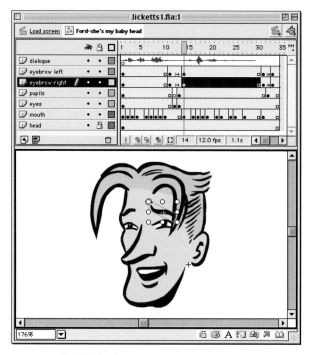

Figure 5.30 Ford's talking head.

For every new scene with facial animation that uses the same head background, you'll need another symbol with that head. Make sure the original head background art is a symbol, instead of duplicating the original head background symbol, place an instance of it in a new symbol and then make the center point the same using the info palette. It's a good idea to not transform the head background within the animated symbol. Otherwise, you'll have heads of varying sizes, and it can get confusing later if you want to duplicate an existing animated symbol as a starting point.

The animated symbol of the head should have the same number of frames as the scene it is used in. If there is dialogue, make a layer for it (you may want to copy the dialogue layer from the scene, especially if there is more than one keyframe containing dialogue). In the Sound palette, Sync should be set to Stream.

Mouth Off

To do the lip sync, you'll need to have several replacement mouths. Variation in expression aside, you can get away with three or four mouth shapes. You'll need the mouth closed, open, open in an O, and maybe one of the mouth open slightly if you can't scale the open mouth. Any more than that is usually undetectable. It's a good idea to put all the mouths for a character together, one after the other, in the timeline. You can then check to make sure the positions match using onion skinning.

Each mouth shape should be made into a symbol when you're done, with each or mouth shape having the same center point. Place a mouth in a layer in the head animated symbol and then scale, if necessary. Scrub through the dialogue; when you need the next mouth shape, add a keyframe and then swap the symbol for the shape you need. Copy and paste the mouth keyframes when you need them. The advantage of working this way is that you often get a mouth animation pattern of several keyframes (such as mouth closed—mouth open—mouth closed) that you can copy and paste. Lip sync generally isn't a whole lot of fun, so anything that makes it go faster is welcome.

Open the mouth on vowels and hard consonants. These should pop out of the mouth. The mouth usually does not close completely between vowels in a single word. Aim to capture the overall shape of the word as opposed to trying to hit every syllable. Try watching your mouth in the mirror as you say a word faster and faster to get an idea of the word's shape.

> **NOTE** If your lip sync skills are lacking, you'll want to check out the Toon Boom Studio demo at www.toonboom.com. Among other cool features, Toon Boom provides an automated lip sync feature.

Eye Eye, Captain

Make sure your character blinks. This is generally done as a replacement eye much like the mouths. The longer the eyes stay closed, the dumber the character. Use blinks to punctuate speech.

When exactly do blinks occur? According to film editor/sound designer/director/screenwriter Walter Murch in his book *In the Blink of an Eye*, blinking "is either something that helps an internal separation of thought to take place, or it is an involuntary reflex accompanying the mental separation that is taking place anyway." You blink at the instant you get an idea. Elmer Fudd goes hunting for Bugs Bunny. He freezes. The instant he realizes he's been duped, he blinks. Twice.

Much of your character's expressions come from the eyebrows. A slight change in eyebrow positioning or rotation can radically alter the emotions the register on a character's face. This does not mean that exaggeration does not apply to eyebrows, but it does mean you have to position them carefully.

Once the head is animated, go back to the scene and use the Instance palette to change the start frame of each head keyframe to correspond to the correct frame in the head animated symbol's timeline. The first frame of head animation may not be the first frame used in the scene, if you plan to cut on a line of dialogue.

LOOPS

Making an animation loop smoothly is easy if it's done with tweens. Make sure the first and last keyframes are identical. If you play this back, there will be a single frame pause because the last keyframe plays and then the first keyframe plays, and they're both the same. The trick to removing the hesitation is to add a new keyframe just before the last keyframe; then delete the last keyframe.

Here's a typical example. In the file called loop.fla, Hickory Dog's nose is swinging like a pendulum. Open the file, select the exercise scene, then play it and note the annoying pause.

Now let's fix it:

1. Add keyframes at the second-to-last frame for the nose and string, as shown in Figure 5.31. The nose and string stay in the exact same place.

2. Delete the last frame. There should now be 16 frames in the animation, as shown in Figure 5.32.

Play back the looping Hickory Dog nose pendulum. You are getting sleepy. Your eyelids are getting heavy. You will send Twinkle all your money. Now wake up!

Here's another typical example. Let's say you want Hickory's nose to spin in a circle. If you want it to go in a perfect circle, you can use the Rotate property in the tweening palette. Check out the scene called "circle" in loop.fla. There's two identical keyframes of Hickory Dog's nose. The nose has been offset from the center point. The tween has been set to rotate clockwise one time. When you play it back, you'll see that it has the same duplicate keyframe problem. As before, add a keyframe to the second-to-last frame, and delete the last frame, keyframe and all.

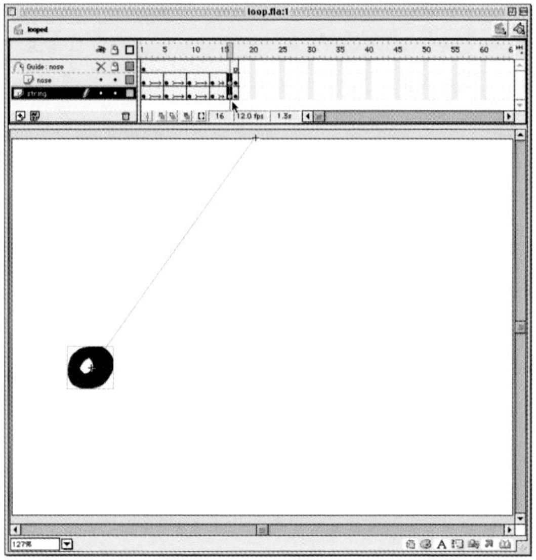

Figure 5.31
Add the new
keyframes just
before the
last frame.

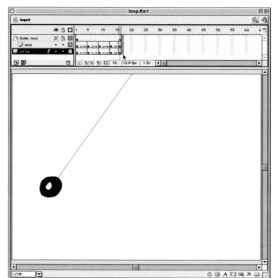

Figure 5.32 Delete
the final
keyframes, and
you'll achieve a
smooth loop.

But when you play this back, the nose spins way too fast. In fact, it goes around twice instead of once. In the tweening palette, change the rotation to clockwise zero times. That's more like it.

Suppose a perfect circle isn't good enough, and you want Hickory Dog's nose to follow a motion path in a loop. If you set two identical keyframes on a motion path, nothing will happen. See for yourself in the scene called "path" in loop.fla. You could move one of the nose symbols over slightly, but Flash tweens will always pick the shortest distance between points. You need to force Flash to make the nose travel the loop, and you can't do that while the loop is enclosed.

1. Pick a start point. Using the Arrow tool or the Eraser tool, make a small break in the motion path, as shown in Figure 5.33.

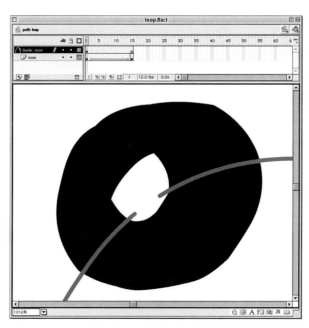

Figure 5.33 Just a little break.

2. With Snap To Objects on, move the nose symbol at the last keyframe to the other side of the break in the motion path, as shown in Figure 5.34. Hickory Dog's nose should now be flying around on the screen.

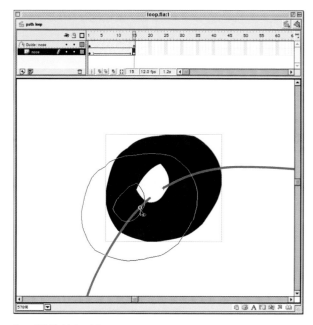

Figure 5.34 Right about there.

3. You may need to adjust the position of the nose in the end keyframe depending on the length of the tween. Using onion skinning will help you here (Figure 5.35).

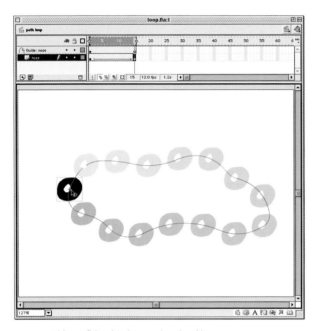

Figure 5.35 Hickory's flying, looping nose in onion skin.

THE WALK CYCLE

Creating a good walk cycle could be the single hardest thing to do in animation. The concept of the walk cycle is to create a looping animation of two steps (both feet) of a character's walk (Figure 5.36) and then move that repeating loop across the screen. That way you only need to animate two steps (instead of however many steps it takes for your character to walk across the screen). Hence, the walk cycle is an animated symbol of the character walking in place, and you tween the animated symbol from point A to point B. Think of it this way: The walk cycle animated symbol is like a person walking on a treadmill; then you drag the treadmill across the screen. The trick is to drag the treadmill at exactly the same rate that the person on the treadmill is walking.

Figure 5.36 Ford shuffles along.

Walk This Way

A character can sometimes be defined by the way they walk because how they walk says a lot about who they are. Have you ever sat around waiting for someone and recognized that person coming from far away, even though you couldn't see their face? Chances are you recognized the way the person moved, and the attitudes conveyed by the way people carry themselves. You might also have seen people who looked similar to the person you were looking for, but ruled them out because they walked differently.

If you have no idea what we're talking about, and even if you do, go out and watch people walk. Notice the differences in the way they move. How much do they swing their arms? How high do they lift their feet? Do they walk fast or slow? Heavy steps or light? Big steps or small? Bouncy or steady? Elegant or idiotic?

Figure 5.38
Carefully trimmed.

Break Down the Drawing

The Twinkle walk cycle method starts with a single drawing. In this case, it's Peculia from the Fantagraphics comic book series *Evil Eye*, created and drawn by Richard Sala. Figure 5.37 shows the original panel, while Figure 5.38 shows Peculia isolated from the background.

Peculia ©2000 Richard Sala

Figure 5.37 A panel from *Evil Eye #1*.

This drawing of Peculia is a good one to start from because she's drawn in an extreme pose with both legs extended. We'll only have to draw back in some of her arms and a little bit of each leg. An exploded view of Peculia is shown in Figure 5.39, all colored and ready to go. Each part is a symbol and on its own layer. In this case, we're not planning on having her bend her arms, so they're single pieces. With a different character (or situation), it might be a good idea to break the arms at the elbows.

Open up the WalkCycle.fla file from the CD-ROM and select the exercise scene. Figure 5.40 shows the symbols that make up Peculia's front leg, meaning the leg closest to the viewer. Right or left can be confusing, but one leg will definitely be in front of the other. Note the placement of the leg pieces within the symbol to put the pivot point where the joint would be. The thigh should rotate near the hip, and the lower leg should rotate at the knee. The arms have their pivot points at the shoulder.

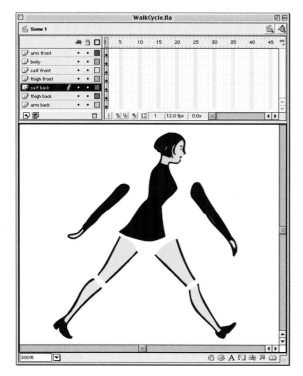

Figure 5.39 A vaguely grotesque exploded view.

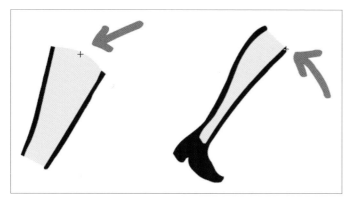

Figure 5.40 Just like real body parts—so fancy!

Here's the first keyframe with Peculia posed and ready to animate. As you can see in Figure 5.41, Peculia's forward leg is planted on the ground with most of her weight on it. Her body is at the lowest point in the walk cycle in this frame, and her arms are at the extremes of their swing. The body has been rotated forward to sell the idea that she's placing weight on her forward foot.

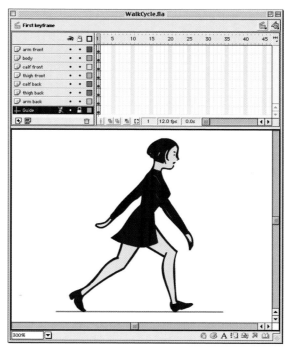

Figure 5.41 Remember: *Animation is exaggeration.*

TIP If you're using the Preston Blair walk cycles for reference, start with the second drawing from the left, not the first. The second drawing shows the character at the lowest point, and should be your first key pose.

Peculia is a confident, tough-but-cute gal, so she has a big stride. Her arms swing nice and wide. She really knows where she's headed, or at least acts like it. If, on the other hand, she were meeker and just out for a little stroll, she might look more like Figure 5.42.

Figure 5.42 Same digital puppet, different attitude.

Keep Those Feet on the Ground

Note the conspicuous horizontal red line in these illustrations. The red line is a guide so you can be sure that Peculia's feet are connecting with the ground. It's crucial to keep feet locked to the ground—this lends weight to your characters.

Make a symbol that consists of a short, 0.5 point vertical line. Add two layers (label them "Guide Line Back" and "Guide Line Front") to your walk cycle, and place an instance of the line in each layer. Align one with the toe of each foot, as shown in Figure 5.43.

You'll use these lines to make sure the feet move on the ground at a constant rate. (While the different lines are red and blue here, the color doesn't really matter—the lines won't be shown in the final movie, only while you're in the testing stage.)

Figure 5.43 The mysterious little blue toe lines.

Once again, think of the walk cycle as a side view of someone walking on a treadmill. They're walking in place. Now, with the person walking on the treadmill, drag the treadmill along the ground—that's basically what we're going to be doing in Flash. We're going to make an animated symbol of Peculia walking in place, as though she were on a treadmill, and then move that animated symbol across the stage, as though we were dragging the treadmill across the stage. The trick is to drag the treadmill at the same rate the person is walking on the treadmill; otherwise, they'll be floating and, heck, anyone can do that.

Here's how we use those little guidelines.

Set another row of keyframes at frame 7. You can adjust this later to make her walk faster or slower, but frame 7 is good for now. Now change her pose so that the opposite leg is forward, and vice versa. Same with the arms. You can adjust her body a bit, too, if you don't want her walk to be too symmetrical. If you choose to do so, make sure you select the body and both arms and rotate them all at once, so the arms' pivot points stay in the same place relative to her body. Make sure the toes of each foot are aligned with the guidelines.

If you're grumbling about how much manual adjusting you're having to do because the knees aren't connected to the thighs, lets say it again: Animation isn't for sissies. You might be thinking that it would be a better idea to make a symbol containing the thigh and calf and then animate the calf rotation within that symbol. That sounds good in theory, but it's nearly impossible to predict where that foot will end up, and it's mighty important to keep those feet on the ground. Just bite the bullet and set those keyframes.

Back to the guides. Copy the first frame of Guide Line Back and paste it into frame 7 of Guide Line Front. When you add a tween, the Guide Line Front should move from the toe of the front foot to the toe of the back foot. The guide lines show you exactly where the toe has to be at each frame of the walk cycle. This distance must be the same for each leg. Copy and paste frames 1-7 of Guide Line Front and paste them into frames 7-13 of Guide Line back. Put a blank keyframe in frame 8 of Guide Line Front and then delete the line from frame 1 of Guide Line Back.

Now copy the first keyframes of the body parts and paste them into frame 13. This will make a complete cycle, but with a duplicated first frame. That's necessary for now. Now put a

motion tween between all the keyframes (Figure 5.44) and play your movie.

Figure 5.44 Ouch. What's up with those knees?

So far, our walk cycle isn't too impressive. That's because Flash takes the path of least resistance when tweening. Motion tweening is a handy function, but it usually only gets you part of the way there. The rest is up to the animator. This is you.

More key poses are needed. You have the two extremes. In between the two extremes, Peculia should have her weight completely on one fully extended leg and be standing straight up while she brings her other leg forward. So set keyframes for all the body parts at frame 4 and set that pose. It should look something like Figure 5.45.

Figure 5.45 That looks better!

Keep the toe aligned to the guideline. Raise her body up (make sure you move the arms with the body) and straighten out the leg she's standing on. Don't worry about the other leg too much. Just get it in the air, ready to be planted on the ground; then set her in a similar pose at frame 10. If you want, you can copy your keyframes from frame 4 for the arms and body. But make sure to adjust the pose a bit to keep her from seeming too robotic.

You might want to lock and/or hide whichever leg you aren't currently working on. And make sure that knee is in the right place! If you want, get the knee in place, rotate the lower leg so the leg is straight and then shift select the thigh so you can rotate them both at the same time. You'll have to reposition the thigh, but at least the knee stays locked in place.

When you play this back, you should have a halfway decent walk. It'll at least give you a general idea of what the walk cycle

will look like. If Peculia doesn't look determined enough, now's the time to fix it by adjusting the key poses. You can give her a bigger spring in her step, or keep her more level for a no-nonsense walk. You might want to make her stride longer or shorter. In theory, you should be able to visualize what your final animation will look like from your key poses.

Scrub through the animation frame by frame (you can use the < and > keys or the controller), and you'll be able to pinpoint the problem areas. At frame 5, Peculia's forward leg should be getting ready to be planted on the ground. So let's grab our keyframes for the forward leg and move them to frame 3. Then at frame 6 add keyframes for the forward leg and straighten it out in anticipation of hitting the ground, as shown in Figure 5.46.

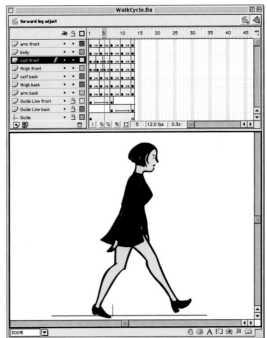

Figure 5.46 Getting more complex.

Do the same for the back leg: Shift the keyframes from frame 10, move them to frame 9, and pose the leg at frame 11 to anticipate hitting the ground. The heel shouldn't be too far off the ground, and should be extended at least as far as the extreme poses. That way, Peculia will look like she's putting her full weight on the forward leg when she plants it. Play it back and see.

Your walk cycle should be shaping up nicely now. There's some tweaking necessary to keep the feet on the ground and aligned with the guides, and also to keep those knees in place. Don't be a keyframe sissy!

Put a keyframe for the "calf front" at frame 2 to put the knee in place, but at frame 4, the forward leg is touching the ground when it should be off the ground (can't always trust that tweening). You'll want to put in keyframes for the whole leg at frame 4 to get the leg off the ground.

Do the same for the other leg, Scrub through your animation, and make sure your knees are in place for the leg you've been working on. When those are done, start in on keeping the opposite feet on the ground and aligned to the guides.

You'll have to put keyframes in at frame 2 and frame 6. At frame 2, you'll want her leg to start straightening out a little more; that should take care of frame 3, but you may want to do more individual tweaks. At frame 6, the foot was going below the guideline, so you'll want to bring the leg up and rotate it a little (Figure 5.47).

The same issues apply to the other leg, so you'll want to put keyframes in the same places. Playback looks pretty good, but the arms need a little work. Give them a little weight by having them slow down as they reach the extremes—adjust the easing on the tweens (Figure 5.48).

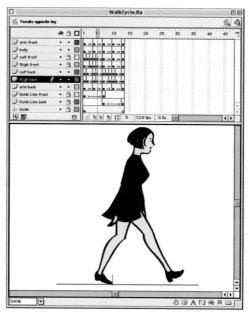

Figure 5.47
Tweaks,
opposite leg.

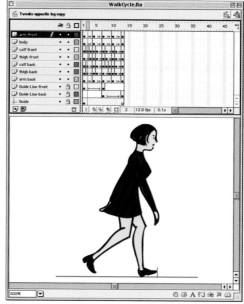

Figure 5.48
More tweaks.

You'll want the arm to start slow and then speed up between frames 1 and 4—that means easing in (Figure 5.49). From frames 4 to 7, you'll want the arm to start fast and then slow down, so that means easing out. Start with 80 for both, and adjust it later as necessary. Do this for both arms, both swings.

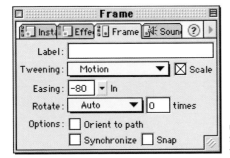

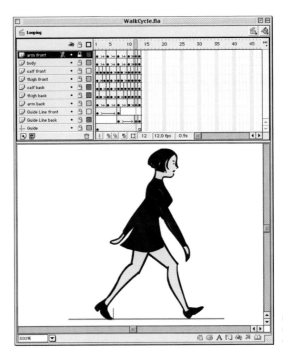

Figure 5.49
Set the easing with the Frame palette.

Figure 5.50
Get ready to loop.

Peculia's body should come down quickly to emphasize the weight she's putting on her forward leg, so set the easing to -60 between frames 4 and 7, and 10 and 13. For the opposite motion of her body going up, ease out by 40. Depending on your character design, this might pose a problem with keeping the shoulders in place, but because Peculia is almost entirely black, it doesn't show. Easing really helps take the stiffness out of Flash animation.

Now you can get rid of that annoying repeated frame, and make the walk cycle loop properly. To do that, simply add a row of keyframes at frame 12 (Figure 5.50). When you delete frame 13, you'll have a perfectly looping 12-frame walk cycle!

To make Peculia walk across the screen using this looping walk cycle, select all the frames, copy them, make a new symbol (graphic), and then paste the frames into that new symbol. It's a good idea to make a symbol of the original animation (before you made it loop) as a backup in case you want to adjust the walk cycle later.

Make a new scene, or get rid of the Peculia walk cycle in the scene you were using, and drag the Walk Cycle symbol from the Library (Figure 5.51) onto the Stage to one side.

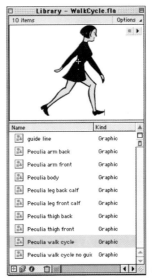

Figure 5.51
The Library.

Now set another keyframe somewhere down the timeline, and drag Peculia to the other side of the screen. It's a good idea to hold the Shift key down when you drag her so she'll walk horizontally. Put a motion tween between these two keyframes, as shown in Figure 5.52, and play your movie.

That looks pretty good (Figure 5.53), but Peculia's feet are shifting on the ground. Fortunately, we have those handy-dandy little blue guidelines at the feet; you'll use those in conjunction with onion skinning to keep her feet locked to the ground.

Figure 5.52 Peculia, from here to there.

Figure 5.53 The walk in onion skin.

Zoom in on Peculia's foot, as shown in Figure 5.54. Chances are the blue guidelines are spaced apart.

You'll want to have the blue lines on top of each other. You can do that by moving Peculia (make sure you're on the last or first keyframe), and/or adding frames. Do both, as shown in Figure 5.55.

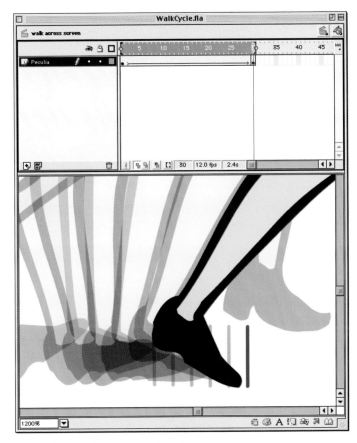

Figure 5.54 The guide lines come in handy again.

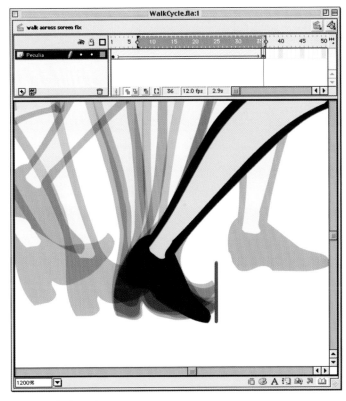

Figure 5.55 Line 'em up!

Once you add some frames, the last keyframe now has Peculia on the wrong frame of the animated symbol. You can figure it out by counting (the keyframe is on frame 36 and the symbol is 12 frames), or you can simply add a keyframe on the frame before it and use the Instance palette to see what frame it's on (Figure 5.56).

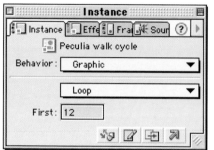

Figure 5.56
Check the frame with the Instance Properties palette.

Delete the keyframe. Click the last keyframe and in the Instance palette change the first frame to the frame number you just learned plus one (in this case, frame 12).

Now play back the movie. Peculia should have her feet firmly locked to the floor with a nice sturdy, determined walk. Go back into your animated symbol, and either delete out the guidelines, or make those layers into Guide layers, as shown in Figure 5.57.

Figure 5.57
Use the Layer Properties palette to change the layer type.

You may prefer to leave them in as guide layers (Figure 5.58), because chances are you may use that walk cycle more than once; then just turn the guide layers back into normal layers, line up the blue guides, and Bob's your uncle.

Figure 5.58 Guide layers are your friends.

But wait…is Peculia plodding a little too heavily? Is her stride overreaching? Make another walk cycle. You've got the setup. Just duplicate the animated symbol, delete all the frames except the first, and start over. Change her attitude. Make her walk tentative, sleepy, wacky, snooty, what-have-you (Figure 5.59).

The Sneak

The key to the sneak is to keep the weight off the forward foot—this keeps the floorboards from creaking. The sneak is also slower than a regular walk cycle. The forward foot must point down and roll onto the heel to absorb the weight as it reaches the contact position. The body should go up and down quite a bit, and it's not a bad idea to actually lean backwards to emphasize keeping the weight off the forward foot. The sneak requires lots of exaggeration. Figure 5.60 shows Richard Sala's Judy Drood doing the sneak.

Figure 5.59 See that? You're making cartoons!

Figure 5.60 Judy Drood, Girl Detective being sneaky. Art originally from *Evil Eye Number 4*.

The Run Cycle

A run is not a fast walk. During a run cycle, the body actually lifts off the ground completely. A run is like a series of hops. The arms swing much more than in a walk cycle, and the body leans forward. You don't need to worry about using the guidelines and keeping the feet locked to the ground as you would with a walk cycle because the distance covered between frames is indeterminate. Figure 5.61 shows Judy Drood doing a run.

A fast run is usually done in four frames: on the ground right foot, off the ground, on the ground left foot, off the ground. However, a fast run would always be animated on ones. In Flash, you can often get away with just using two frames, though, because the frame rate is usually much slower than that of film. The trick is to make sure that each frame is sufficiently different so that when it is played back, the legs appear to be flailing. If the poses are too similar, the legs will not seem to be moving at all, or worse, the legs will look like they're going backwards like wagon wheels in an old western. The arms should not swing at all. Figure 5.62 shows Hickory Dog doing a fast run in two frames. If you like, add some extra legs with alpha transparency to simulate blur, or motion lines.

Figure 5.61 Richard Sala's Judy Drood makes a run for it.

Figure 5.62 Run doggie, run!

Make Every Keyframe Count

A tween requires a start and an end keyframe. But it is often the case that a symbol is on the Flash Stage unmoving for a while, and then it tweens. Instead of repeating the exact same keyframe as the start of the tween, adjust it a little. Move it in the opposite direction for instant anticipation. You have to set the keyframe anyway, so make it count.

There will also be many times that a character or chunk will go from being onscreen to off screen, or vice versa. Instead of keyframing the chunk to be completely off screen, use the keyframe to control the last bit of the chunk you'll see (or the first, if it's going from off screen to on); otherwise, the Flash tween picks what part of the chunk you'll see last, and it may not be the greatest. This is especially important if the item rotates on the way in or out. Add a blank keyframe afterward to clear the item off the Stage. Make those keyframes count!

BRUTE FORCE, PERSEVERANCE, AND PIXIE DUST

With enough brute force, perseverance, and pixie dust, your digital puppets will become believable characters. The little details make all the difference. In the next chapter, you'll get the gospel of story, characters, storyboards, animatics, acting, and dialogue, as you prepare to create your animation.

6

Now What?
Character and Story

The previous chapter laid out techniques for animating characters in Flash based on classic character animation principles. But that's all they are: techniques. All the technique in the world will get you nowhere unless you have a story to tell, and characters with which to tell it. A good story can be made better with great animation; however, the greatest animation on earth can't save a bad story. Let's move away from the Flash how-to for a while, and get back to the theory behind it all.

You've seen this many times—super-slick animation with technique up the wazoo, and it's boring as hell because the story just isn't interesting. Or it's a halfway decent story with characters you just don't give a crap about. It happens in movies all the time, especially effects-heavy movies where it seems like the filmmakers just thought up a bunch of cool effects scenes and then strung them together. Now, it's true that Hitchcock made *North by Northwest* that way. He had a bunch of ideas for action sequences, and it was up to Ernest Lehman to string them together in a plausible manner. And they made a classic. Most of the time, this doesn't pan out too well for a feature film. Oddly enough, this method *does* work for cartoon shorts, provided you have great characters to support it. More on this later.

While you can come up with your own working methods, the workflow that most animation studios use goes like this:

1. Create story and characters
2. Storyboard
3. Create an animatic (a video storyboard) with scratch dialogue
4. Edit animatic
5. Record dialogue with real actors as scenes are finalized
6. Create animation according to animatic

Notice that animation comes last. Each of the previous steps is equally important as the actual animation. But first and foremost are character and story.

TIP   You'll probably want to watch the cartoons on the accompanying CD-ROM before driving too far into this chapter. (They're located in the Jicketts folder.)

THE TWO MOST IMPORTANT THINGS (not necessarily in that order)

There are two things that every great cartoon has: compelling characters and an exceptional story. As the song says, just like love and marriage, you can't have one without the other. Compelling characters can make up for a mediocre story, and an exceptional story can make up for mediocre characters. But you've got to have some of both. Before you set a single keyframe in Flash, you must have the best possible story, and the best possible characters with which to tell the story. Otherwise, all the effort you put into your animation will be for nothing.

Do yourself a big favor and read Syd Field's book *Screenplay*. As you might guess from the title, it's about writing screenplays, which you might think has nothing to do with your cartoon. The same things that make great movies (such as story and character) also make great cartoons.

Character

Characters are defined by what they do, not what they say. Let's say you've got a lumberjack. He can stand there and say, "I'm a tough guy," and all the audience can do is choose whether or not to believe him. But if you drop a log on the lumberjack's head, he might cry like a baby or brush it off with a single sweep of his mighty hand. Whichever he does, there is no question as to how tough he really is.

Generally speaking, cartoon characters don't have to be especially well-rounded, or as actors like to call it, "complex." They can be completely one-dimensional, as long as that single dimension is a good one. Boil the character's essence down, exaggerate it, and you've got the makings of a great cartoon character. Now, that's not saying that cartoon characters can't be just as fascinating as a complex, nuance-filled performance by Sir Lawrence Olivier. It's just not likely, and doesn't play to animation's strengths—especially not in the short form dictated by the Flash medium.

Think of a great cartoon character and then ask yourself, "What is this character?" You can usually come up with several things, but one trait will rise above the rest and define that character. Bugs Bunny is many things, but mostly he's a smart-aleck. Elmer Fudd is many things, but mostly he's an incompetent hunter. Donald Duck is cranky. Goofy is goofy.

One good method for coming up with characters is to fill in the blanks of this phrase: [name of character] is a [occupation] who is [trait].

Using some Twinkle examples, "Hickory Dog is a mutant hillbilly dog-man who is really stupid," or "Ford is a hot-rod hoodlum who is naïve but means well." If you can't sum up your character this way, you don't know your character well enough.

Character Types

If you need help coming up with character occupations, check out Chapter 7 of Gene Deitch's online book *How to Succeed in Animation* at http://genedeitch.awn.com/. While you're at it, read the rest of the book. It's chock-full of valuable information and insights from an industry legend.

Whaddaya Want?

The next thing you need to know about your character is: What do they want? This is referred to as *dramatic need*, and tends to be specific to the story. If the character doesn't want anything, they have no reason to be doing anything, and you end up with a dull cartoon.

A character's dramatic need can be a very simple one, and it can change throughout the course of the cartoon. But it must always be clear what it is. What is Wile E. Coyote's dramatic need? To get the Road Runner. Within each scene in the cartoon, the immediate dramatic need can vary (such as he needs to get across the ravine, or he needs to save himself from drowning), but these result from or lead back into his dramatic need.

Define your character first; then fill in the blanks of this phrase: [name of character] is a [trait] [occupation] who wants to [dramatic need].

"Hickory Dog is a really stupid mutant hillbilly dog-man who wants to satisfy his hunger."

"Ford is a naïve but well-meaning hot-rod hoodlum who wants to get the girl."

Note that you're not going into specifics here. You must boil the need down to its most basic so that the dramatic need it is absolutely clear to you. Only then will you be able to communicate that need to the audience. It's easy to get distracted by the details that seem so darn funny at the time. If those details fail to serve the fundamental dramatic need, they have no business being in your cartoon.

Hickory Dog spends his screen time in "I'm Hongry" chasing a chicken. His most pressing need is to satisfy his hunger, and trying to catch the chicken is how he attempts to fulfill that dramatic need. There are any number of things Hickory Dog could have done to

In this corner...For those who can't be bothered to check out the CD, here's Ford standing up.

satisfy his hunger. He might have gone to the 7-11 and bought a Snickers bar, but then he'd have to find a 7-11 and scrounge up some money. He might have searched for roadkill and cooked up a stew, but then he'd have to avoid traffic and deal with the broken well pump. Satisfying hunger is Hickory Dog's dramatic need. How he goes about it is the story.

Story

The fundamentals of storytelling can be summed up with a nursery rhyme:

> *Little Miss Muffet sat on a tuffet,*
> *Eating her curds and whey.*
> *Along came a spider,*
> *And sat down beside her.*
> *And frightened Miss Muffet away!*

The first two lines establish who she is (the *protagonist*) and what she does. It's not very ambitious, but it's unmistakable. The third line introduces the *antagonist*, or "the bad guy." Not every story has a bad guy per se, but there is always something or someone who gets in the way of what the protagonist wants. That's called *conflict*, and is established in line four. The fifth line is the *resolution*. In this case, it might not be a particularly satisfying one, but it's an ending nonetheless. There's not much extraneous detail in this nursery rhyme. It really doesn't matter what Miss Muffet's eating, but otherwise it's the absolute essentials of the story, and has everything a story needs:

1. Protagonist
2. Conflict
3. Resolution

You can start with a character and then come up with a conflict to put the character in, or you can start with the conflict and then develop a character to fit. If you start with the character, first define the character, and their dramatic need. Come up with ways to keep the character from fulfilling that dramatic need; then come up with a way for the character to achieve the dramatic need in a way that is surprising yet satisfying to the audience. This is much harder than it sounds.

If you start with the conflict or situation, one good technique for finding a suitable protagonist is to come up with the least-qualified character to deal with the conflict. This makes it easier to come up with obstacles to the dramatic need; then come up with a way for the character to achieve the dramatic need in a way that is surprising yet satisfying to the audience.

It's a good idea to come up with the ending first. This is not as crazy as it sounds. First of all, it's easier to get somewhere when you know where you're going. Your cartoon can have great characters as well as a great situation to put them in, but if the ending flops, the whole thing will fizzle. If you know your ending, your obstacles or gags can build on one another. Otherwise, the conflicts might seem random or unfocused.

If you know your ending, you can save the best for last. Walt Disney used to do this. He'd have the "gag men" come up with humorous situations, and the funniest one would be the final gag. Then they'd come up with other gags to lead up to the final one, which they knew would be the funniest. That way, the cartoon has a good payoff, like a punch line to a joke.

Once you've decided who's going to be in your cartoon, what the conflict is, and how it gets resolved, you can start piling on the details. You know what's going to happen, so now you can figure out how. Good characters and a good situation can lead to many different conflicts and resolutions, even if they're just variations on a theme. The Road Runner shorts are all have the same story: Wile E. Coyote tries to catch the Road Runner and fails. The *what* is the same; it's the *how* that changes.

This is where story is truly created, and there's nothing that can be said to help you. Telling a good story is the hardest thing in the world (especially a good *funny* story), and no one has the secret formula for it. Otherwise, every movie you see would be good. Every joke you hear would be funny. Your parents wouldn't be boring. Sorry. That's just how it is.

TIPS OR CLICHÉS? YOU MAKE THE CALL

Your English professor may have hung you out to dry for using too many clichés, but we're talking 'toons here, not literature. If you think we're just listing a bunch of clichés, you wouldn't be wrong. But there's a reason why clichés exist: They keep on working. In a cartoon world, clichés can be tips. Chances are your cartoon will be only a few minutes long, and you will have much to communicate in that short period of time. Using time-honored traditions will help the audience grasp quickly what you're getting at. Besides, we'd rather see classic cartoon gags over yet another bad George W. impersonation any day. Also, you can use the cliché expectation to turn the idea on its head. What if Wile E. Coyote stepped off the cliff, blinked at the audience, cringed, and then *never fell?* He just walks back over to the cliff and scratches his head. But that joke only works because the audience expects one thing, you set them up for more of the same, and then pull the rug out from under them.

Establish Characters and Conflict ASAP

Until the audience knows who they're watching and why, they'll just be twiddling their thumbs. The story cannot begin until it has been properly set up. An audience wants to be told a story, so don't make them wait too long. However, it is a common error to start out a cartoon or movie with the main characters talking about themselves, trying to explain who they are or what the plot is. At this point, the audience doesn't have a reason to care about the characters, so no one will listen to what they have to say. Instead, establish the characters and the conflict quickly through actions. Show the audience who the characters are and the situation they're in. Save the exposition for later when you have the audience's full attention. And when you're done telling your story, don't overstay your welcome.

Endear the Protagonist to the Audience Early

Win the audience's sympathies, and they'll follow you anywhere. A good way to do this is to embarrass your character, because everyone can relate to embarrassment. How your protagonist reacts to an embarrassing situation is a good indicator of character. A great example of this is the opening sequence of *Harper*, where Paul Newman makes the world's most disgusting cup of coffee and then drinks it. The key, though, is that Harper, Paul Newman's character, gags and spits it out. In *End of Days,* Arnold Schwarzenegger drinks the world's most disgusting breakfast drink, but he doesn't seem to mind. Apparently, that shows what a tough guy he is, but who can relate to that?

The protagonist must take the active role, and as they say in *Highlander,* "There can be only one." Even if you've got a duo, one is always dominant. The protagonist should initiate events— cause them to happen, not just react to them.

Conflict

In a "good guy vs. bad guy" story, it's a good idea to make the antagonist way bigger/stronger/tougher/smarter than the protagonist. If it's too easy for the protagonist to defeat the antagonist, what's the point?

The three basic conflicts are Man against Man, Man against Nature (or Machine), and Man against Self. Of course, "Man" does not specifically mean male, or even human. But these are your range of choices when it comes to picking an antagonist, and they'll help define the characters' conflicts and obstacles.

When coming up with conflicts for your character to face, try the old "good news, bad news" routine. The good news is the protagonist finally made it to the top of the cliff; the bad news is his triumphant "YES!" started an avalanche. Giving your character little victories along the way helps keep the audience involved in his or her plight. Remember, luck always runs out, particularly at the moment protagonists think they've got it made. Keep raising the stakes. The more good news they get, the more they have to lose.

Make Sure Every Scene Is about Something

Every scene should do at least one of the following: Advance the plot, develop character, and/or make the audience laugh. If not, it doesn't belong in your cartoon. Two characters are sitting at a table talking. Ho hum. Put a ticking bomb under the table— now the scene is about something. That particular example is Hitchcock's explanation of suspense. There are two critical factors: The audience must know the bomb is there, and the bomb must not go off. Dramatic irony, where the audience knows something the characters do not, really keeps the audience involved in the story. The bomb must not go off—certainly not before one or both of the characters realize(s) that the bomb is there—because that would be the wrong kind of release of tension, and the audience would never forgive you.

Give the Characters Something to Do

If there are two characters having a conversation, put them in a careening bobsled. Or have one of them trying to swat a fly. Or make one character need to go to the bathroom really badly. Giving the characters something to do gives the scene a dynamic, and allows you to reveal character.

Try painting your character into a corner. Get your character into a situation where you can't possibly think of a way out, and then think of a way out. This will force you to come up with a creative, surprising solution. If it surprises you, it'll probably surprise the audience, too.

Make Sure the Story Is about Something

We don't mean that your cartoon has to have a moral, but it should have some sort of overall concept that it is trying to get across. Subtext, if you will. It doesn't have to be a big, important issue. It'll usually boil down to something like "might makes right," or "love conquers all." The moral of "I'm Hongry" is "stupid is as stupid does," or something like that. If you know what your story is supposed to be about, you'll have an angle on the action, and it'll be more clear what fits and what doesn't.

Your story should be about the most important thing that ever happened to your protagonist. If it's only moderately important, or the second most important thing, you're working on the wrong story. The events have to be so important to the character that they're important to the audience, too. According to the theory of character arc, the events of the story should be so important that they forever change the protagonist. However, we're talking about short cartoons, not plays or feature films, so we feel that this can safely be ignored. If you're working on a cartoon series, it's a little more like television where the characters change slowly over the course of many episodes, thus keeping the viewers involved. It's true that every Road Runner cartoon has pretty much the same story. Chasing the Road Runner is the most important thing that ever happens to Wile E. Coyote. It's not like he's working on a cure for cancer in his spare time.

Give the Audience a Way In

Your cartoon can take place in Psychedelic Insanity Land, but it might be best to make the protagonist the one normal person who finds him or herself in that strange place. The audience will have an easier time relating to a character they immediately understand. Besides, it provides the story with contrast. If everything is strange, nothing is strange. But in Psychedelic Insanity Land, everything is strange to the one sane person there. The other side of this is no matter how strange or fantastic the world your cartoon takes place in, the story should probably be about the one time things were different. Again, it's an issue of contrast. Something strange or different must happen in even the most strange or different world in order for the audience to understand what that world is normally like (which is strange and different). This is especially true for science fiction and fantasy stories, where it is critical that you first establish the "rules" of that world.

Ever watch a movie and leave the theater (or rewind the videotape) thinking, "That movie had no story!" Chances are the movie actually did have a story; otherwise, it would have been a series of totally random events (which has been known to happen). What's more likely is this: The plot did not require the characters. In other words, the events that occurred in the movie could have happened to anyone, not specifically the characters in the movie. It didn't matter who the characters were, or the events didn't matter to the characters.

Luckily, Hollywood spends zillions of dollars each year to teach you these lessons. They're called Just Okay movies. Good movies need no fixing. Bad movies are beyond fixing. But Just Okay movies have some things right, and some things wrong. You can try to figure out what the wrong things are, or at least know not to use that combination. It's always an unproven theory, because you can't really remake the movie to fix it and see if you were right. But speculation doesn't cost anything. If you come up with a really good fix, you can change a few elements and then turn it into a cartoon.

Funny Doesn't Come in the (Flash) Box

How to be funny is another thing that can't be taught. There's no secret formula or plug-in we can give you. Funniness can only be judged by the audience. What one finds hilarious another may not. All you can really do is put forth what you think is funny, and hope someone watching agrees with you. With that in mind, there are a few things that are generally true about being funny, though it's easy enough to find exceptions.

Most comedy situations involve a deception of some kind. Whether it's men dressing up as women to hide from gangsters or trying to produce a surefire Broadway flop, the element of deception works much like suspense, because the audience is in on something the other characters are not. The protagonist has something to hide from the other characters, and gets into deeper and deeper trouble due to this deception. But unlike the ticking time bomb under the table, this bomb must go off. The deception must be revealed, or the audience will never forgive you. If the antagonist is doing the deceiving, the comeuppance is the best part.

It's much funnier watching things go wrong when you know the plan. This is similar to the deception rule, except it's not the characters holding out on each other, it's fortune. The audience has to know what the characters are supposed to be doing to laugh when they can't do it.

There's no payoff without setup, and the payoff must come at the right time. We've all heard jokes where the person telling the joke botched the punch line. Chances are the joke was fine, but the timing of the punch line was off. Sometimes the difference between funny and not funny is a single frame. That's the critical nature of timing.

Violence without consequence is funny You can drop an anvil on a character's head, or have one chop another to bits with an ax, or blow them up real good. Just make sure that in the end, nothing really bad happens. This is the secret to slapstick. Think of all the Saturday morning cartoons you've seen where the characters beat the crap out of each other. At worst they see stars, grow a lump, or say "Yeowch!" But there's never any blood. That's a different joke based on shock value, and shock value only works once. *Itchy and Scratchy* on *The Simpsons* walk this fine line between clever and stupid, and what makes them so outrageously funny is that it's violence with slight consequence. Like they say, "It's all fun and games until someone gets hurt."

The impossible is funny because reality is the setup You know that if you walked off a cliff, you'd fall. So when Wile E. Coyote walks off a cliff and doesn't fall, it's funny. You know something he doesn't, which is that he should fall, and it's funny watching him realize this. When he finally does fall, he eventually hits the desert floor, and violence without consequence is funny.

Truth is funny When the observation that a joke makes rings true and the audience recognizes something they've observed, it resonates and gets a much bigger laugh. Feel free to pick an obscure truth. There's a moment in *For Love or Money* when Michael J. Fox orders in some Chinese food and then tosses the packets of soy and duck sauce into huge bowls full of the same packets. Like the binder of delivery menus, anyone who's ever lived in New York knows what it's like to have tons of those packets, whether or not they keep them. Maybe a joke like that won't play as well in the People's Republic of Togo, but so what if not everyone gets it? If you miss, you miss. But if you hit, you hit big.

Extreme exaggeration is funny This can again only happen in contrast to the cartoon's level of normality. Ren is normally a calm asthma-hound Chihuahua, but when he freaks out, he REALLY freaks out. Or like the baseball player who swings so hard he twists himself into a knot, the more he twists, the funnier it is. You really can't exaggerate too much in cartoons.

Embarrassment at a character's expense is funny Embarrassment at the audience's expense is not. This is why sex can be funny, but love never will. When characters are embarrassed, it's funny to watch them squirm, as well as being a great revealer of character. But just as violence should be without injury, embarrassment should not cause any permanent damage.

Funny comes in threes This is a kind of setup and payoff, often taking the form "same—same—different." Do it once to set up the joke. Do it twice to make the pattern clear. Now the audience expects one more, but you give them something different. And since they now come to expect that the third one will be different, the anticipation actually makes it funnier.

Make one the straight man Again, the comedy comes from contrast. If everyone's crazy, then no one's crazy. But if there's one sane person to judge the craziness against, you've got the ingredients for comedy. There are countless comedy duos where one's the straight man and the other's the funny one. But how many comedy duos can you think of with two straight men? Or two funny ones? It's all about the contrast. Also, it's good to have a voice of reason so the comedy proceeds on a vaguely logical basis.

LOVE THE SHOW

Love the Show

Students of comedy, tune in to WFMU (91.1FM, Jersey City, NJ or listen to the audio stream at www.wfmu.org) on Wednesday nights from 6 to 7 pm to hear the funniest radio show on earth. Hosted by station manager Ken Freedman and screenwriter Andy Breckman *(Rat Race, Sgt. Bilko), Seven Second Delay* is an audio train wreck not to be missed! Check out the homepage (www.wfmu.org/7sd/) for archived shows, and say The Benediction every day before you work on your Flash cartoon.

STO-RE-BOARDING

The ace storytellers at Pixar call the storyboarding process "sto-re-boarding" because they rework the scenes so many times. But that's how they come up with such great stories. Two of the four years they spent making *A Bug's Life* were devoted to honing the story. All the animation in the world can't make up for a lousy story.

A storyboard is a series of sketches that indicate what will happen in your cartoon. There should be one new drawing for each major change or action in a scene. When you look at them in sequence, the actions should be clear with little or no dialogue.

The storyboarding process is where you "write" your cartoon. Forget about scripts. All you need are a few paragraphs outlining the characters, events, and resolution; then start drawing. Tell the story in pictures. Work out what happens visually. If you need dialogue to explain what's going on, you're not telling the story in pictures. Animation is a visual medium.

Don't Say It if You Can Show It

This is harder than it sounds. Writing can be very abstract. It all takes place in the mind of the reader, where blanks can be filled in, connections can be made, and a few words can encompass many actions. It's easy to write, "Mooney sets the phone on fire." But how exactly does that happen?

As it turns out, the answer is: Mooney calls Pizza Stop and then tries to hang up the phone using the torch because he's too short. He accidentally hangs up the torch instead of the phone, and goes back to work with the phone in hand. He tries to spark up the phone, and when it doesn't light, he cranks up the gas. He tries again, figures his sparker is busted, and tosses it over his shoulder where it hits the telephone and then lights the torch, setting the phone on fire. Character animation cannot be abstract. Each action must clearly show the audience exactly what is happening, one action at a time. That's why it's no use trying to write down a cartoon. Write it with storyboards!

At Twinkle, we like to draw our storyboards on blank 3 x 5 index cards, and tack them to the wall in order. That way, they can easily be shuffled around, new drawings can be swapped out, and it's easy to get an overall idea of where the scene is headed. Don't spend too much time on the drawings—just get the idea across. Besides, it could change at any moment.

And change they will. At this stage, it's easy to try different approaches, or riff on an idea that a drawing sparks. It's also the time to find out what works and what doesn't. It's much better to toss out a few index cards than to toss out final animation because you just couldn't get the scene to work. If you suspect something isn't working, you probably won't be able to fudge it in the animation.

Storyboarding is where you work out your key poses. Careful storyboarding will help you figure out where you can reuse drawings, parts, and backgrounds. Try to maximize the use of a single drawing, even if it's in a totally different scene.

Use the Language of Film

Even though there's no movie camera in Flash, you should act as though there were. There's a firmly established language of film that you can use to tell your story. Most people are reasonably fluent from the cumulative experience of all the movies they've seen. But, as anyone who's ever tried to learn a foreign language knows, it's one thing to understand a language when you hear it spoken, and another thing entirely to be able to speak it or write it. Check out *The Five C's of Cinematography* by Joseph V. Mascelli for a good crash course. It applies directly to the staging of your animation, and will affect how you storyboard. Instead of setting up a camera for a shot, you'll be building that shot with animation on the Flash stage. You'll compose the shot the same way, pick the angles, and choose when to cut just as you would if you were making a film.

Want a Real Camera?

The lack of a movie camera is one of Flash's biggest shortcomings as a serious character animation tool. That's one of the reasons that US Animation's fabulous Toon Boom Studio is so compelling. With Toon Boom, you can fly your camera through a three-dimensional stage; the pans and zooms made possible (not to mention fast and easy) might blow your brains out in Flash.

Establishing Shot

Where in the world are your characters? An *establishing shot* is often used at the beginning of a sequence to set the scene and orient the audience to that locale. At a glance (as shown in Figure 6.1), the audience can see that Ford has pulled up in front of Jickett's Speed Shop.

Figure 6.1 An establishing shot: Jickett's Speed Shop.

Master Scene

If your cartoon were a movie and you filmed an entire scene that occurs in one location from start to finish, that would be called a *master scene*. Later you would shoot different angles of the actors in the scene and cut them in. Just as the establishing shot show the audience where they are, the master scene shows the audience the action between the characters. It shows the audience the physical space, and where the characters are in relation to that space. Take a look at Hickory Dog and his beloved chicken in Figure 6.2. Even if you never end up using a master scene in your cartoon, you have to know what it would look like if it existed.

Figure 6.2 A master scene: Hickory Dog and the chicken.

Long Shot

We're not talking about that outside chance in the eighth race at Belmont Park. A *long shot*, in cartoon terms, takes in the whole scene. It's shot from the blimp, or maybe the roof of a tall building. In many cartoons, the initial establishing shot is a long shot that works into a pan or zoom.

Medium Shot

The *medium shot* usually shows the characters from the waist or knees up. This allows your characters to move freely without having to make walk cycles. It's close enough to see facial animation, but far back enough to capture gestures. Think of the camera set up for a TV news anchorperson and then back the camera up a bit.

Two-shot

The *two-shot* is a specific type of medium shot that shows two characters. Figure 6.3 shows a typical two-shot. Well, maybe it's not *that* typical. What the heck is Hickory Dog doing talking with Ford?

Figure 6.3 The two-shot: Hickory Dog and Ford.

Close-up Shot

The *close-up is* one of the five C's of cinematography. Close-ups are native to film, and can be a powerful storytelling device. Use a close-up to isolate an action and draw attention to its significance. It's a mechanism to burn a point into the retina.

Over the Shoulder Shot

The *over the shoulder shot* is a common type of close-up, with specific rules of continuity to follow. Draw an imaginary line between the characters. This is referred to as the *action axis,* as depicted in Figure 6.4. You can show any angle of the characters in a 180-degree arc on one side of the line. But when you change the camera angle to be over the other character's shoulder (the *reverse angle*), the camera may not cross the axis or the new angle will confuse the audience. The idea is to keep the characters on the same side of the screen when changing camera angles. Figures 6.5 through 6.7 show the right and wrong way to transition to a reverse angle.

Figure 6.5 *An over the shoulder shot: Angel and Ford.*

Figure 6.6 This reverse angle stays on the correct side of the line.

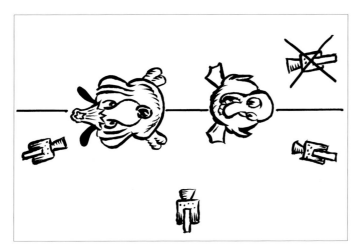

Figure 6.4 The action axis, bold as love.

Figure 6.7 This reverse angle "crosses axis," and is confusing when cut together with Figure 6.5.

Cut In Close-up Shot

The *cut in close-up* is a magnified portion of the preceding larger scene that continues the main action. A common example of this would be a shot of one character during a conversation. The action axis still applies, and, more importantly, the eyes must look in the correct direction. This means you must be clear on the physical locations of your characters in relation to each other. Figure 6.8 shows a cut in close-up shot of the torch that Mooney uses to put the phone back on the hook (or not). You can check this out in the scene-by-scene rundown in Chapter 9.

Figure 6.8 A cut in close-up shot: Watch that torch.

Pan Shot

A *pan shot* moves the camera view along a landscape. Figure 6.9 shows a *tracking shot,* which is a specific type of pan that follows a character. As the character moves, the camera moves with her, as shown in Figure 6.9. As Peculia walks along, the camera remains fixed on her, while the street scene slides along. Flash's lack of a true camera requires that you move the background (and foreground) object(s).

Figure 6.9 A tracking shot: Peculia struts down the street.

Zoom Shot

A *zoom shot* does exactly what you think it should: The camera zooms into a specific point of interest within a larger scene. Once again, the lack of a camera in Flash makes you play tricks. In this case, you'll scale up the objects in order to create a zooming effect.

DIALOGUE

The problem with dialogue is that it takes time to say things. Because your cartoon will probably be only a few minutes long, the more your characters talk, the less time they have to do things. Animators refer to cartoons that are all talk as "illustrated radio," and nothing is more inexcusable. To make a cartoon of characters standing around talking defeats the entire purpose of animation, but, sadly, people are used to this idea because of cartoons made for television. One way to judge this is to ask, "Does this really need to be animated? Would it work just as well if it were a sitcom/home video/roll of toilet paper?"

Storyboard your cartoon first. Tell the story in pictures. Don't say it if you can show it. If you're having trouble with a story point, solve it with dialogue only as a last resort. Instead of having your character say, "Boy, I'm tired," think of some way to show how tired they are, such as the old "propping open the eyelids with toothpicks" gag. Dialogue is just icing. Any words that come out of your characters' mouths should do at least one of the following:

- Advance the plot
- Develop character
- Make the audience laugh

Except for purely expository dialogue, try not to have the characters say what they mean. Only children and morons say exactly what's on their minds. It's much more effective when the audience knows what the characters are trying to say, but are unable or unwilling to. It's about what *isn't* being said. You can establish this through body language, the preceding scenes, and familiar situations. We had a heck of a time coming up with the right dialogue for Ford's flirtation with Angel at the end of the *Jickett's Speed Shop* pilot. It wouldn't do to have Ford walk up to her and say, "I think you're hot. Wanna go out on a date?" Ford had to be boastful without being obnoxious, and Angel had to be insulting yet alluring. In the end, Daniel Clowes saved the day by coming up with dialogue and a situation that reveals so much about the characters and what they want, even though they're talking about their cars and racing.

BUILDING THE ANIMATIC

Once the storyboards tell a complete story with clear actions, you add time. The animatic is your chance to see if your cartoon works before you commit yourself to animation. In short, the animatic is a rough cartoon with scenes and sound, but sans animation. Using a video animation program, whether it's Flash, After Effects, Premiere, Final Cut Pro or whatever you have, put the storyboards together with temporary dialogue and music, and work out the timing. If the story doesn't work in the animatic stage, there's no way it'll work with final animation.

Scan the Final Storyboards

It's a good idea to number the scene drawings in case you accidentally knock a stack off the table, but then again if you can't put your scene back together by looking at the boards, you probably don't know your scene well enough. A descriptive naming convention helps. If you're going to use Flash for your animatic, save the scans as .png or .gif files so the file names are preserved.

Record Scratch Dialogue

Record your initial dialogue quickly and cheaply using your own voice or anyone else who's easily available. Edit it quickly using the sound-editing program of your choice. At Twinkle, we use Bias Peak for all sound, from recording to editing to sweetening. Eventually you'll get real actors to do the voices, but for now you want to work out the timing, and make sure all the dialogue is necessary. It's important that you be able to make changes easily, so doing it yourself is a good idea. Music clearance rights are a tricky issue, but find some music that's close to what you want. Animating to music is surprisingly helpful.

Place Storyboard Scans into a Video Editor

Next, you'll take those scanned storyboards, and assemble them in a video editing software application. We prefer Apple's Final Cut Pro for animatic work (rather than Flash), because Final Cut Pro is specifically designed for video editing, but you can get the job done plenty of other ways. If you choose to do build the animatic in Flash, you'll drop the scans into the timeline in sequence, and adjust the timing by spacing the keyframes. You can do rudimentary camera moves and transitions, but mostly you should concern yourself with timing. Do a run-through without any dialogue at all. Try to tell the story without any words—just the storyboards and timing. You might be surprised at how little dialogue you need (and how much time dialogue eats up).

At this point it will become clear whether any storyboards are missing. Perhaps you need an insert close-up to clarify a story point, or an establishing shot of a location. It should also start to become apparent if a scene or bit of business isn't working or is unnecessary. Now is the time to fix it. Rethink it. Draw it again. Plug it into the animatic. If it doesn't work now, it'll never work when you animate it.

When the animatic makes sense and tells the story effectively, you can then add the scratch dialogue and temp music, and get used to repetition. You'd better love your dialogue and be sure it's absolutely critical to your cartoon, because you'll be hearing it over and over again. Lines you thought were hi-larious when you recorded them will cease to be funny. Your neighbors will hate you. Toss out any dialogue that isn't essential. Actually, you should toss out anything that isn't essential, but especially dialogue. Don't say it if you can show it.

EDITING

Editing animation is different than editing a movie. When you make a movie, you go out and shoot all the scenes at different angles, with different takes, and lots of different set-ups. You then go into the editing room, and put all those bits and pieces together into a coherent sequence of events. With animation, you edit first into a coherent sequence of events and then make the pieces. You don't want to make any more pieces than is absolutely necessary because it's so darn time-consuming, so you figure out exactly what you need before you start animating.

Juxtapose

The other purpose of editing is to tell a story. This is done in editing by juxtaposing images. Suppose you have two images, one of a gun firing and another of a woman screaming. Neither one by itself tells much of a story. But put the two together: A gun is fired; then a woman screams. Now you have a story where previously none existed. Reverse the two: A woman screams; then a gun is fired. Now you have a completely different story using the same two images. This is the power of editing.

Whenever possible, tell the story in juxtapositions. This requires the audience to make the connections between the images, which connects them to the story in an immediate way by making them participants in the telling of the story. It also allows you to cut down on the amount of actual animation you have to do, or the number of new pieces that need to be drawn.

For example, we could have shown Ford being insulted by the Old Man at the convenience store, glumly taking his beer and change, shuffling over to the door, glancing back at the Old Man with contempt only to receive another withering look, pulling on the door only to discover he has to push, pushing the door, and walking through. Or we could have the Old Man insult Ford, and cut to an exterior shot of Ford walking out of the convenience store. The point is that Ford feels like a schmuck.

The first option is a lot of exposition explaining (in pictures) how Ford gets out the door. The second option leaves the image of the Old Man insulting Ford in the minds of the audience and goes straight to Ford outside, walking away from the convenience store. The audience makes the connection that this is the same store where he was insulted, and that he must have walked out through the door. The audience knows how a door opens, and how one walks through a door. They don't need to be shown. Unless it gets across a story point, or develops character, it's unnecessary. Or as the hot rodders say, *"If it doesn't make it go, it's gone."*

Let it Fly

While music video–style editing, with all its quick cuts, has really changed movies for the worse, it works great for Flash animation. By telling your story with a juxtaposition of quick, singular actions, you can maximize your use of a single pose, minimize the amount of character animation you actually have to do, and still tell an effective story.

This leads to another general editing rule of thumb: start late and end early. Going back to the scene of Ford in the convenience store, obviously for Ford to be there at all he had to get in somehow. So instead of starting with him putting the can on the counter, we could have backed up and shown him parking his car, getting out, walking up to the AfterMarket, opening the door, going inside, getting the beer out of the refrigerated case, walking over to the counter, and then putting the can on the counter. But it's unnecessary. All that stuff happened—we just chose not to show it. We started late in the scene. And then there's all the stuff after the Old Man insults Ford, which also happened, and we also chose not to show that. We ended the scene early and let the audience fill in the blanks. Better to keep the story moving.

Editing is choosing pieces and assembling them in the right order. Editing is telling a story through juxtapositions. And editing is creating a rhythm. There's an inexplicable magic that occurs when you add a music track to something you've edited together. Certain things will just fall into place as though you had timed them to the music. It's a good idea to edit to music because it helps you establish a rhythm to your cuts. This does not mean that you must cut every four bars. When to cut is largely a matter of feel, and the right music can help you get that feel. If you don't have the final tracks you'll be using in your cartoon, pick something close to it.

Another critical element to creating a rhythm in editing is contrast. Action scenes tend to have many quick cuts. Dialogue scenes tend to have fewer, longer cuts. But you don't want a cartoon that is all quick cuts any more than you want one that is all long cuts. Contrast the cuts and create a rhythm.

Want to Understand Editing?

Stop watching television. TV editing is very different than movie editing, and it's a good idea to get away from the television style of editing, particularly in the way dialogue tends to be handled. This is mostly because TV shows must be shot quickly and with few takes and setups, whereas movies are planned out carefully with many takes to choose from. So watch movies instead—movies generally considered classics. Pick a sequence and study it carefully. Try to predict where they'll cut. It's harder than it sounds. Eventually you'll get the rhythm of the scene.

Notice when they cut during dialogue:

- Is it at the beginning of a new line of dialogue, or on the end?
- Is it on a particular word?
- Is the emphasis on the speaker or the listener?

It's actually impossible to tell what went into the editing of a movie. Who knows why the editor cut at that particular moment? It could be because it felt right, and it was an artistic decision. Or it could be that was the only take that hadn't been ruined by the lab. Or some screwball extra kept looking into the camera.

With cartoons, you have total control over what's going to be on the screen, because it hasn't been made yet. Choose your shots. Pick your angles. Base your choices solely on what best serves the story. Be prepared to get rid of anything that doesn't belong. Even that joke that cracks you up every time, but just slows the whole thing down. Toss it. Use it in another cartoon. Don't worry about including a shot you have no idea how to execute. If it's the best way to tell the story, use it. Figure out how to do it later—it'll force you to be creative. The flip side of trying to reuse pieces as often as possible (as with a typical Flash modus operandi) is to create a new piece whenever necessary. If the story calls for an angle of a character that will only be seen once, so be it. And don't be afraid to use it for just a few frames.

DIRECTING

When people think of directors, they usually imagine a guy who yells "Action!" and "Cut!" a lot, but that misses the point of what a director does. The director's job is to make choices. A movie director spends most of the day answering questions. Those answers directly affect what goes on the screen. The same goes for directing cartoons. The director doesn't have to do all the work, but does have to make choices about the work that gets done, and who does it. A director needs to have a specific vision—a direction—for the animation, and needs to be able to communicate that vision.

Know Your Craft

If you're going to direct a cartoon (even if you're directing yourself), you've got to know your craft. Remember being forced to read Shakespeare in high school? You might not have enjoyed it then, and you may not enjoy it now, but it was good for you—the literary equivalent of eating your vegetables. Fortunately, cartoon vegetables are pretty tasty. After all, most of them are designed to make you laugh. So study the classics. Watch as many as you can. Find an animator who influences you and then find out who influenced that animator. Study the great physical comedians, like Charlie Chaplin, Buster Keaton, the Three Stooges. Look into the history of animation. The more you know, the more you can draw upon when you make your own animation, which leads to the next important point.

Steal from the Best

No matter what idea you come up with, someone else has already thought of it. Nearly everything has been done before, so don't bother trying to reinvent the wheel. Because there are so many wheels out there, get to know them, borrow bits and pieces from the ones you like, and make your own wheel out of them. Or take an idea and run with it. Just make sure that when you steal, steal from the best. It's no use ripping off something that's lame to begin with. The more you know, the more you have to steal from. You don't have to limit yourself to cartoons. Steal from film, theater, literature, music, anything. Especially film. Just steal from the best.

> **NOTE** Uhhhh … We're not talking about *stealing*, we're talking about borrowing concepts and treatments in a referential and reverential manner. You should always respect copyright.

Know the Rules Before You Break Them

It goes against the entire spirit of jolliness that cartoons ought to have to say there's anything you shouldn't do. Go wild. Knock yourself out. Break all the rules. But break them consciously. Do so from a position of choice. Your audience will thank you for it.

Act It Out

To really understand a scene, you've got to act it out. You've got to get to the bottom of what the scene is about. What drives the scene? (Remember the scene with two characters sitting at a table with a bomb underneath?) Performing the scene will help you figure out what it's about, what the actions are, how it should be timed, and how to stage it.

You can't know how best to stage an action if you're unclear on the action itself. And because character is action, acting out the scene will help you figure out how your characters will perform those actions. When you've got a clear understanding of the actions and how they will be performed, you'll know what to exaggerate. You'll also understand the physical space the action requires, and that will give you a better idea of how to stage the action. You'll then know where to put your characters, the best angle to view them from, and what backgrounds you'll need. It's one thing to think up a funny bit of business. It's another thing to storyboard it. And it's something else entirely to perform it. Sometimes what seems so clear in storyboard form makes no sense once you act it out.

Perhaps you feel you've never done any acting before. Ever look someone in the eye and lie? That's acting. You can do it. Now, we're not talking about "what's my motivation" acting (although it is a good idea to know your characters' motivations). We're talking about cartoon acting, which is broad and almost entirely physical. This is why we recommend studying silent film comedians. They perform broad, clear actions—without dialogue—in the real world, or at least one that physically exists. Animation is an exaggeration of such actions and staging. Animation is acting. When you animate a character, you're performing. You're creating a performance through a character. Otherwise, you're just moving stuff around on the screen.

Directing Actors

We strongly recommend hiring professional actors to do the voices for your cartoons. While Billy West might be out of your price range, there are actors with day jobs in every town, and most of them are glad to practice their craft for minimal compensation. Because you've removed all but the most essential dialogue, why waste it on a mediocre performance? When you bring in actors, they'll have their own ideas about the characters, some of which may never have occurred to you. You'll have slaved away over the material for an eternity, while they'll see it with fresh eyes. Plus, while you're recording the dialogue, you can watch the actors' gestures and mannerisms, and get ideas for the characters.

The thing actors seem to say most about directors they like is that "they know exactly what they want." A really good actor just needs to be pointed in the proper direction, but if they need more information, you'd better have the answer. They'll want to know the same things an animator would want to know. What's the scene about? Who is the character? What is the character doing? If they need further direction, try to give it to them in terms of actions. If the scene has the character annoying another, instead of telling actor to be an obnoxious screwball, tell them to annoy the other character. Or provoke, offend, or taunt the other character. Remember, character is what you do, not what you say. And it's not what you say, it's how.

Most actors don't mind reading lines and doing one half of a conversation, but some prefer to have someone to react to. If you have a dialogue exchange to record and you have all the necessary actors at the same time, you can record them together. When it works, it works great. But it had better be exactly what you want, because it can be extremely difficult to edit afterwards.

Aside from knowing what you want, the most important thing do when directing actors is to *listen*. Sure, you'll have ideas about what the character should sound like. But listen to the actor. Don't just listen for what you want to hear, because you'll be shutting out a world of nuance and possibility. Know exactly what you want so you'll be prepared for the unexpected when it occurs, and you'll know how to use it. A good actor can make a character come alive before any animation begins, and it makes the job of character animation that much easier.

THAT'S A WRAP!

You won't always follow the same route to create a great cartoon. That having been said, this chapter should serve you as a road map, rather than a set of directions. Study that map. Watch the cartoons. With a little luck (and a whole lot of hard work), you'll always have a fun place to go, an interesting voyage, and great characters to get there with.

7 Building Scenes

Now that you've laid all the groundwork, it's time for the jolly part—making the animation. One of the great things about animation is that it offers you the ability to choose exactly what goes on the screen. The drawback is that you don't get anything for free. Everything the audience sees has to be created. But if you plan carefully, you can keep the number of elements that need to be made to a minimum and still have plenty of flexibility with your characters.

Layout is key step. Disney's *Illusion of Life* suggests four methods to plan and layout a cartoon:

1. *Thoughtful Thumbnail*—small sketches drawn from the storyboards, quickly revised in pursuit of continuity.

2. *Traditional*—a painstaking approach that nails down each scene with more complete drawings.

3. *Multiple Choice*—meant to prod the participants into creative action, this method lets you pick and choose between the possibilities.

4. *Long Shot* or *Establishing Shot*—a master image provides an encompassing landscape from which to plan. With a wide-angle view, you'll know where everything is located in the scene.

The Twinkle approach borrows a bit from each of these methods. This chapter gets into the mechanics of layout as it dives into the topics of backgrounds, scene building, camera moves, and transitions.

BACKGROUNDS

The act of creating backgrounds is like theatrical set design, except you can choose where the audience looks. Backgrounds are a large determining factor in how a scene is staged. The perspective at which a background is drawn dictates the "camera angle" of the shot. Once you know the camera angle (perspective) of the background, you can determine the angles at which the characters must be drawn. If the perspective of the background and characters (or inanimate objects) fail to match, the sense of reality may suffer.

Backgrounds must be detailed enough to clearly present the location without distracting from the action. Colors must be chosen carefully to allow the characters to contrast with and stand out from the backgrounds. Muted, relatively monochromatic color schemes tend to work best; however, brighter colors can be used in a particular area as a kind of permanent spotlight to frame the action.

It is often the case that making a background larger than is required for a single scene will allow you to reuse the background elsewhere. If, for example, the background is substantially wider than a shot requires, you can use a different section of it in another scene, perhaps with a change in brightness or tint.

TIP It's not a bad idea to pick a target screen size, whether you use bitmap or vector background art. Scaling up an animation with a bitmap background usually results in a loss of quality. Scaling up an animation with a vector background might look pretty much the same; however, the larger the screen size, the slower the movie plays.

At Twinkle, we like to use painted backgrounds because everything in Flash has a hard edge. The softness of watercolors gives the scenes depth; the backgrounds stay back. Watercolors often hold up well to enlargement and JPEG compression. And just as importantly, it's the classic cartoon look. When we use Flash chunks in the background, we make sure that none of the lines are black to soften up the image and distinguish it from the characters.

Bitmap Hazards

Bitmap backgrounds can pose a few problems. They can add to your file size, and because of this, they limit the size of your playback. You may have heard the party line that says that bitmaps are bad for Flash work. While there's some weight to this argument, to be sure, it's a horrible thing to restrict your work to vectors through-and-through. For more hints with bitmaps in Flash, check out these two TechNotes on Macromedia.com:

Bitmaps shift in Flash:
www.macromedia.com/support/flash/ts/documents/bitmaps_shift.htm

Flash Player Streaming and File Optimization Techniques:
www.macromedia.com/support/flash/ts/documents/flash_stream.htm

BUILDING A SCENE

There's any number of ways to build a scene, but here's the Twinkle workflow:

1. Start with the background.
2. Add characters and then put them in their first key pose.
3. Adjust the composition to best stage the action.
4. Add foreground elements.
5. Add more key poses, and "make it nice."

We might switch the order of steps 3 and 4 depending on how the foreground items get used in the scene, but basically that's how it works.

Start with the Background

Suppose you want to build a scene with Hickory Dog and the chicken. Figure 7.1 shows the background bitmap placed on the Stage. It's hard to tell exactly where it's going to end up in the frame, so we're going to make a mask to cover up anything outside the frame. Start with the file **scene.fla** from the CD-ROM.

Figure 7.1 Here's a pastoral scene, just begging for a mutant dog.

In this corner…A multiplane camera move.

1. Open the exercise scene, and create a new layer named mask. In the mask layer, draw a rectangle the size and position of the Stage area. Use the info palette to ensure it's the right size and in the right place. The upper left corner should be at 0,0 (Figure 7.2). Change the dimensions of the rectangle to match the movie. Group the rectangle. This will be the "hole" in your mask.

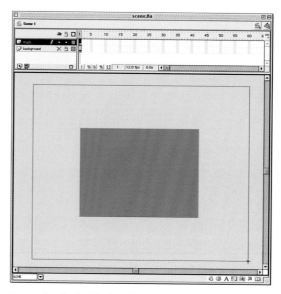

Figure 7.3 Drawing the big ol' masking rectangle.

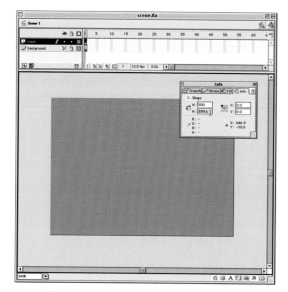

Figure 7.2 The dimensions of the first rectangle should be the same as the movie.

2. Pick a different color than the one used in step 1. Draw another much larger rectangle covering the entire Stage, as shown in Figure 7.3. This is the mask. Because it isn't grouped, it will automatically go underneath the grouped hole rectangle.

3. Break the inner rectangle apart and then deselect it. Double-click the inner rectangle to select it and its stroke (if any), as shown in Figure 7.4.

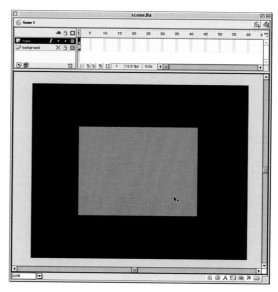

Figure 7.4 The inner rectangle selected.

4. Delete the inner rectangle and then group the mask. Label the layer, and lock it (Figure 7.5). Make sure that this layer is always the top layer.

Figure 7.5 The background, masked.

You can now see the exact boundaries of the Stage, which is helpful when testing your movie.

Adjust the position and scaling of the background. If you plan on doing a camera move, make sure you have enough background to go from the start position to the end (and make sure it's a symbol, of course).

Looping the Background

If your background needs to scroll from one side of the screen to the other and continue in a loop, (such as a tracking shot with cars driving), make sure that the background is sufficiently large to keep the loop from being too obvious. Twice as wide as the screen area it has to cover is about right. Make sure to match the ends of the background where they meet, or the seam will show. In the file called **backgroundloop.fla**, there's a background from *Jickett's* that has to travel from left to right.

1. Open the scene named exercise and place the Bkg-Road horizontal background symbol on the Stage, as shown in Figure 7.6. You'll need to scale the background up a bit (109.8%) with the Transform palette. The background should just make it past the right side of the screen. This is the start of the loop. The red lines shown in Figure 7.6 are the outline of the Stage mask.

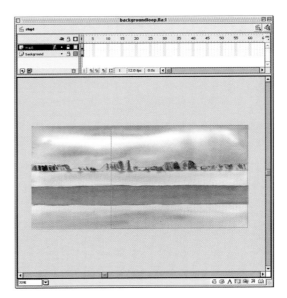

Figure 7.6 Start with a nice wide background image.

2. Set a new keyframe around frame 15. In the new keyframe, hold down the Shift key and move the background to the right, all the way off the Stage. Add a tween (Figure 7.7).

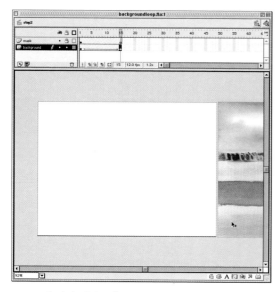

Figure 7.7 Check the timing after you've added the tween.

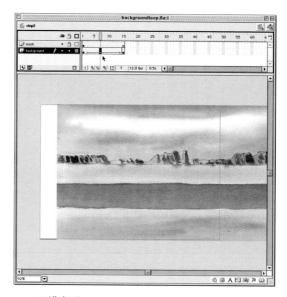

Figure 7.8 All clear!

3. Scrub through the tween until you find the frame where the background first clears the left side of the screen. The frame and position will vary depending on the length of the tween. In this case, it's frame 7, as shown in Figure 7.8.

4. Create a new layer, and name it background 2. Copy keyframe 1 from the original background layer, and paste it into the new layer on the frame you determined in step 3. Paste the same keyframe into the last frame of the new layer (Figure 7.9) and tween.

Figure 7.9 Doubled up.

5. In the frame determined in step 3, move the background to the left until the right edge meets the original background, as shown in Figure 7.10.

Figure 7.10 Try using the arrow keys to move the background.

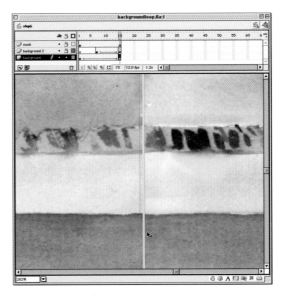

Figure 7.11 Give it a nudge.

6. In the end keyframe of the original background layer, nudge the background until the left edge meets the right edge of the new background (Figure 7.11). Definitely use the arrow keys. Zoom into at least 100% to get this spot on; if you're zoomed out, you may end up a pixel off.

7. If you're satisfied with the timing, add keyframes for the two background layers at the second to last frame, as shown in Figure 7.12. Delete the last frame, and the animation will loop.

Figure 7.12 Almost ready to loop.

The seam is obvious in the previous example, but it helps show you how the looping works. You'll probably want to make this a movie clip and replace it into the background layer. We avoided this problem in *Jickett's* by flopping the background horizontally and then looping it again. Check out the scene labeled "seamless" in the backgroundloop.fla file to see how it works.

Add Characters

The next step is to place your characters in the scene and set the first key poses. The key poses must integrate the characters into the scene, and should be scaled properly to fit with the background. If you haven't already made a digital puppet of the character, import the art into the scene. (Follow the methods outlined in Chapter 3 to create a digital puppet with each symbol on its own layer.)

The order of the layers is important: Top to bottom in the layers equals foreground to background on the Stage. Think of the pieces as being physical objects, like paper cutouts. If a piece needs to go in front of another, its layer should be on top. The more characters you have interacting on the Stage, the more important it is to have your layers in the proper order. If you need to change the layer order of a symbol, simply copy and paste a keyframe into a new layer or an existing layer (or copy and paste in place the symbol); then put a blank keyframe in the original layer.

Figure 7.13 shows a typical example. (Check out the scene 2 scene in the scene.fla from the CD-ROM.) Hickory's outside arm is on the top layer. During extreme poses the leg could go in front of the arm, but other than that the arm should be in front of everything else.

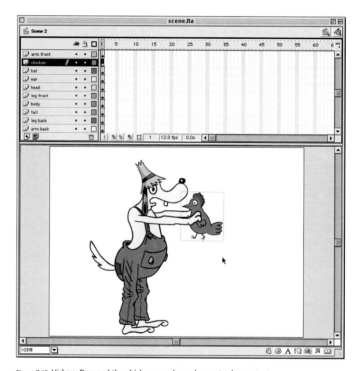

Figure 7.13 Hickory Dog and the chicken are always happy to demonstrate.

Let's take a look at some more situations.

Suppose Hickory drops the chicken and it runs past him, as in Figure 7.14. This works fine because the chicken layer is below the arm, but above everything else.

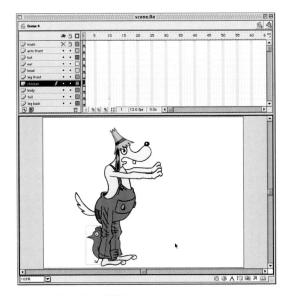

Figure 7.15 Here chickie chickie!

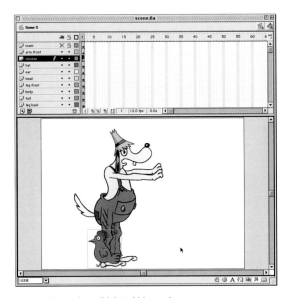

Figure 7.14 Now where did that chicken go?

However, if the chicken needed to run between Hickory's legs, the layer order would have to change so that the chicken is behind the front leg and body, but in front of the back leg. Check out Figure 7.15 for the change in layer order.

Now suppose Hickory starts in this standing position, as in Figure 7.16.

Figure 7.16 Hickory's front arm is in front of the leg, and the back arm is behind the other leg.

But if the chicken runs through his legs and then he bends over to follow the chicken, the layer order will not allow his arms and head to go between his legs (Figure 7.17). To fix this, you'll have to make the chunks swap layers. The front leg will have to go in front of the arm, and the back leg will have to go behind the back arm.

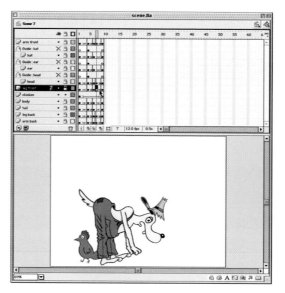

Figure 7.18 Add those keyframes.

Figure 7.17 Whoops! Let's get his head and arm behind that front leg.

Ready to give it a try? Open up the chunk swap exercise scene in scene.fla:

1. Add keyframes at frame 7 to the arm layers. Add keyframes at frames 6 and 7 to the leg layers, as shown in Figure 7.18.
2. Create a new layer. Grab the last three frames of the "arm back" layer, and move them into the new layer (Figure 7.19).

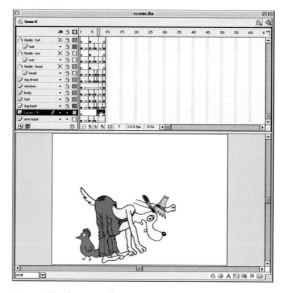

Figure 7.19 New layer, same frames.

3. Grab the last three frames of the "leg back" layer, and move them into the "arm back" layer as shown in Figure 7.20. Move the three frames of the arm from the new layer into the "leg back" layer and then delete the temp layer.

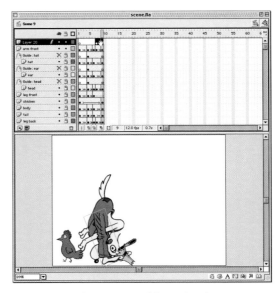

Figure 7.21 The new layer sits on top of the arm front layer.

Figure 7.20 Frames moved.

This layer swapping keeps the number of layers down, which is sometimes helpful. With the outer arm, however, the layer swapping technique won't do because the arm may need to go in front of the head, hat, or ear. A new layer is necessary.

1. Create a new layer above the "arm front" layer. Grab the last three frames of "leg front," and then move them into the new layer (Figure 7.21).

2. Add a blank keyframe to frame 7 of the "leg front" layer so there won't be two front legs (Figure 7.22).

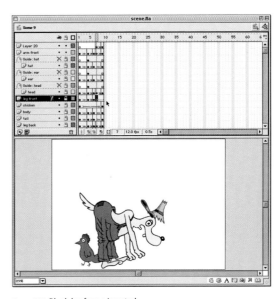

Figure 7.22 Blank keyframe inserted.

Hickory Dog should end up in the pose shown in Figure 7.23. When you play the animation back, this layer switching should not be noticeable at all.

Figure 7.23 He's a limber mutant dog.

Adjust the Composition

Once the characters are in place and the initial key poses are set, figure out where the characters will wind up by the end of the action. You don't have to set the end key pose, but you should have a pretty good idea of where the characters need to be on the screen to perform the actions required.

If the framing of the background will not allow for the range of action the scene requires, now is the time to fix it. Scaling the background may be sufficient (even anamorphically, if necessary), or additional background may need to be created. If the characters' actions are closely tied to the background, scale them and the background at the same time. It may be that the background is fine as is, but the characters need to be scaled or repositioned to best present all the action.

If you have multiple key poses, to scale or reposition them all at the same time, you'll need to use Edit Multiple Frames. Open the adjust composition exercise scene in scene.fla, and follow these steps.

1. Click the Edit Multiple Frames button. As shown in Figure 7.24, adjust the edit range by dragging the Start and End Onion Skin markers to cover the frames you want to change, which could be the entire timeline. If you change the frame you're on, you may need to adjust the Onion Skin markers.

2. Unlock and unhide all the layers you want to adjust. In this case, the Guide Layers need to be unhidden so they can be moved with the other chunks. Select All (Command-A/Ctrl-A). Figure 7.25 shows all of the chunks selected.

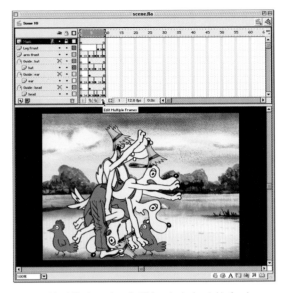

Figure 7.24 Yow! (And you thought Hickory looked weird before.)

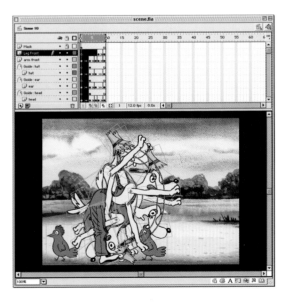

Figure 7.25 That's a lot of chunks.

3. Now you can scale, rotate, and reposition all the keyframes at once, as shown in Figure 7.26. You might want to uncheck the Edit Multiple Frames button to check the positioning of your characters, but be sure to Select All again after you turn Edit Multiple Frames back on.

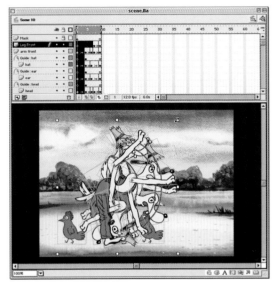

Figure 7.26 Scaled down and moved a bit.

Add Foreground Elements

If the foreground elements play a role in the action, they should be placed with the initial key pose of the characters. Otherwise, they should be placed afterward to help frame the action. Of course, they can also go in the background to give it depth.

If the foreground item is a bitmap image, you need to create an alpha channel for it and then import it as a .png file. An alpha channel tells Flash what parts of the bitmap image should be transparent. But because the alpha channel is grayscale, there are 256 levels of transparency, including completely solid and completely transparent. This means that you can have soft-edged foreground objects. You can even blur them to simulate depth-of-field.

Okay, kids, it's time to jump into Adobe Photoshop for a bit. Rock.png is the file you now need from the CD-ROM.

Creating an Alpha Channel with the Magic Wand Tool

If you can, use the Magic Wand tool to select the area(s) that should be transparent (Figure 7.27). You might need to adjust the Magic Wand tolerance in the Options Palette.

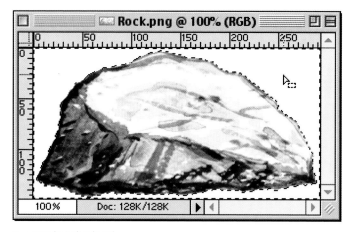

Figure 7.27 The rock, selected.

It's a good idea to enlarge the selection area a little to avoid a halo around the image. The anti-aliasing of the selection is made up of shades of gray, and those translate into varying levels of transparency. You want varying levels of transparent rock as opposed to varying levels of transparent white background. To enlarge the selection area, go to Select > Modify > Expand and then pick a number of pixels to expand the selection area, as shown in Figure 7.28.

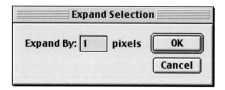

Figure 7.28 One or two pixels should do it.

Choose Select > Save Selection to bring up the Save Selection dialog box. The operation should be New Channel, as shown in Figure 7.29. Click OK.

Figure 7.29 This creates a channel called Alpha 1.

Click Alpha 1 in the Channels palette (Figure 7.30).

Black is transparent and white is opaque, so if the area that you want to be transparent is white (as shown in Figure 7.31), you have two options.

Invert the image (Command-I/Ctrl-I), as shown in Figure 7.32, or double-click Alpha 1 to bring up the Channel Options dialog box. If Color Indicates is set to Selected Areas, switch it to Masked Areas, and vice versa (Figure 7.33).

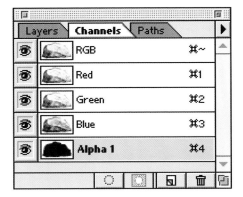

Figure 7.30 The Alpha 1 channel should appear below the Red, Green, and Blue channels.

Figure 7.32 The alpha channel inverted.

Figure 7.31 This *isn't* what you want.

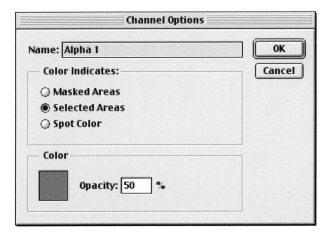

Figure 7.33 The Channel Options dialog box.

Manually Creating an Alpha Channel

In situations where the background is too complex, you can't use the Magic Wand tool. Instead, you'll have to define the Alpha channel manually. In the Channels palette, create a new channel, as shown in Figure 7.34. Turn on the visibility of the other channels, but make sure the Alpha channel is selected. If you start with an all-white Alpha channel, you'll have to fill in the area you want to make transparent with black. If you start with an all-black Alpha channel, you'll have to fill in the area you want to make opaque with white. Open up tanks.psd (from the CD-ROM) in Photoshop.

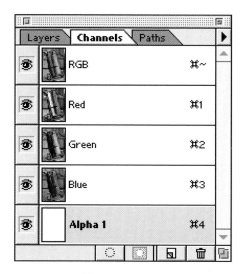

Figure 7.34 A new Alpha channel.

Let's assume you start with an all-white Alpha channel. Make a rough selection of the area you want to make transparent using the Lasso tool (Figure 7.35).

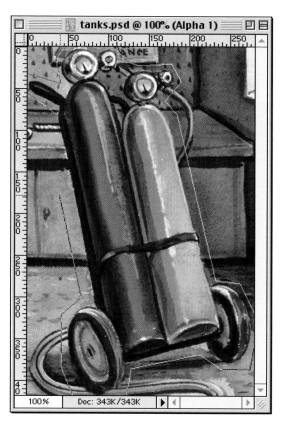

Figure 7.35 A rough selection.

Invert the selection if necessary (Figure 7.36), and fill the selection with black. The Alpha channel will appear as a transparent color, as shown in Figure 7.37 (the default is red with a 50% transparency). To make things easier to see, you can change the color to something with more contrast, as in Figure 7.38.

You can also use the Pencil tool set to black to draw a rough outline of the area you want to make transparent, and use the Paintbucket to fill in the rest. The point is to keep the parts of the Alpha channel that should be solid as solid as possible. Otherwise, there might be semi-transparent chunks floating around your solid chunk.

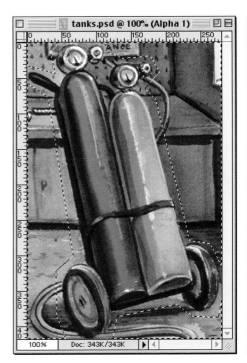

Figure 7.36 The selection, inverted.

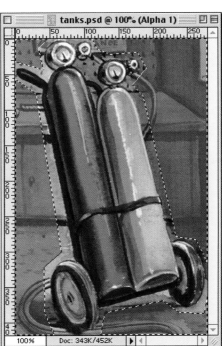

Figure 7.37 If red doesn't provide enough contrast …

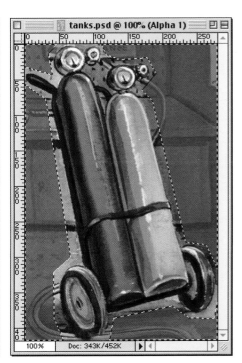

Figure 7.38 … try blue instead.

Use the Paintbrush to define the edges of the Alpha channel, as shown in Figure 3.39. The amount of feathering determines the softness of the edge. For straight edges, click the paintbrush at one end, hold down the Shift key, click the Paintbrush at the other end, and Photoshop will draw the line for you. Make sure you fill in any gaps between your Paintbrush edge and the rough outline.

Save your work as a Photoshop file. If you like, crop the image down close to the edges of the Alpha channel to keep file size down. If you crop or resize the image, however, you may need to go back over the edges of the Alpha channel with the Paintbrush or Pencil tool. Cropping can cause anti-aliasing, which in turn leads to a halo box around the image. Save it as a PNG file and you're good to go. Figure 7.40 shows the rock imported into Flash with an Alpha channel.

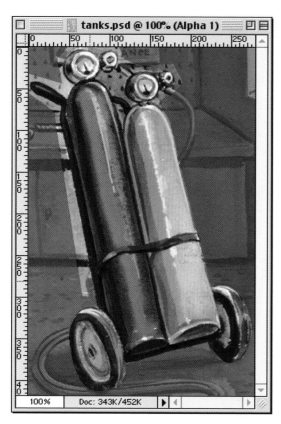

Figure 7.39 Hey, waddya want? It's the manual method!

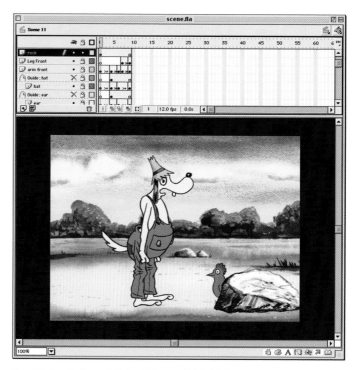

Figure 7.40 Now that's a rock that a chicken can hide behind.

Make it Nice

Now it's time to set additional key poses, make sure the timing is right, and add tweens. Use the arsenal of character animation principles from Chapters 4 and 5 to make your animation jolly. (Use nice.fla from the CD-ROM for all the necessary chunks.)

Flash allows you to tween from one symbol to another. Suppose you have these two Hickory Dog legs, like the ones shown in Figures 7.41 and 7.42. They're the same relative size and have similar center points.

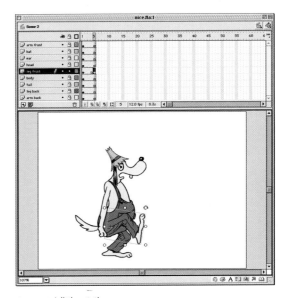

Figure 7.43 Hickory's ready to walk.

Figure 7.41 Leg one.

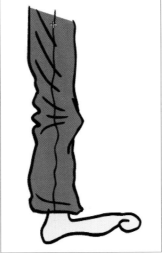

Figure 7.42 Leg two.

Using these two legs and a single tween you can make Hickory lift his leg and kick it straight out, which would be good for a nice stupid walk cycle. Figure 7.43 shows a static Hickory.

1. Select the exercise scene in nice.fla. Add about four frames to every layer. On the leg front layer, add a keyframe at frame 5. At the new keyframe, rotate the leg, as shown in Figure 7.44.

Figure 7.44 A little rotation.

2. Using the Swap Symbol dialog box, swap the current symbol ("leg bent") with "leg straight" (Figure 7.45).

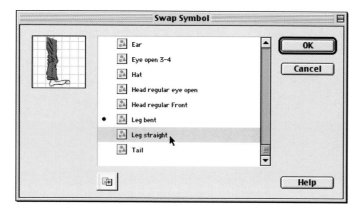

Figure 7.45 Swap those leg chunks.

3. Add a tween, and adjust the straight leg's rotation as necessary. Figure 7.46 shows the tween and swapped leg in onion skin.

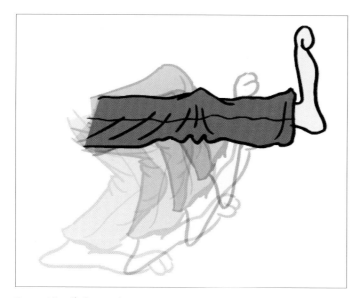

Figure 7.46 Now that's snappy!

Flash allows you to treat an animated symbol as a single-frame symbol by adjusting the symbol's "behavior." You can get a lot of mileage out of a single symbol this way. Suppose you have the animated symbol of Ford's hand shown in Figure 7.47 (Beer-Ford arm). If you place this symbol in the timeline, by default it'll play the animation in a loop for as many frames as there are in the timeline. But you can change this in the Instance palette.

Figure 7.47 Is that an itchy finger?

When the behavior is set to Graphic (even if the original symbol is defined as a Movie Clip), you can specify whether the symbol loops, plays once, or only shows a single frame, as shown in Figure 7.48. You can also specify which frame these start on.

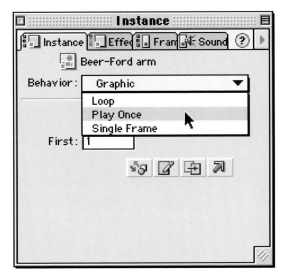

Figure 7.48 Loop, play once, or show a single frame.

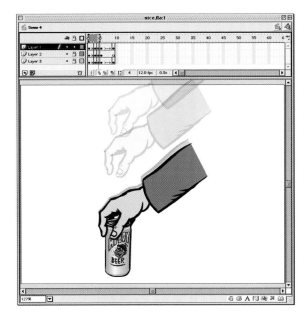

Figure 7.49 Thunk.

In this animation, Ford keeps his fingers on the beer can as he puts it down; then as he takes his hand away, his finger extends. While his hand is on the beer can, the symbol is used as a graphic, set to Single Frame starting on Frame 1 (Figure 7.49). Once he lets go of the can, the symbol is set to Play Once, starting on Frame 2.

This tweens to the same symbol, Single Frame starting on Frame 2, as shown in Figure 7.50.

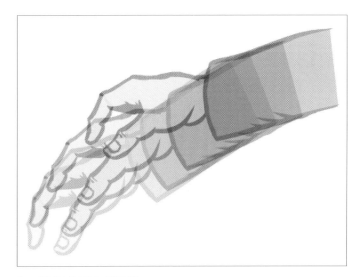

Figure 7.50 The tween in onion skin.

Faster Testing

It's a good idea to test your movie as much as possible; but the more sound there is, the longer it takes to export, and this is a major deterrent. The problem is that the MP3 compression takes a lot of processor time.

The solution is to temporarily change the compression. Go into the Publish Settings and change the audio compression (stream and event) to ADPCM. You can choose Raw if you don't mind larger files. When you're finished, change the settings back to MP3.

COMBINING SCENES

Most likely, you'll be setting up each shot as a separate scene in Flash. Often, several scenes will need to be combined into a single scene, usually due to sound overlapping from one scene to the next. Suppose you have two scenes that need to be combined.

1. Open up the combinescenes.fla file from the CD-ROM. Start with the second scene. Select all the frames across all the layers. If the timeline is large, select the whole column of frame 1, scroll to the end of the timeline, hold down the Shift key, and select the last frame in the same layer you ended on in frame 1, as shown in Figure 7.51. Copy the frames (Option-Command-C/Ctrl-Alt-C).

2. Go to the first scene. Add a new layer and put it at the bottom. In this new layer, paste the frames (Option-Command-V/Ctrl-Alt-V) into the frame after the last frame in the timeline. Unfortunately, the layer names will be lost, as shown in Figure 7.52. Flash creates the new layer names with sequential numbers instead.

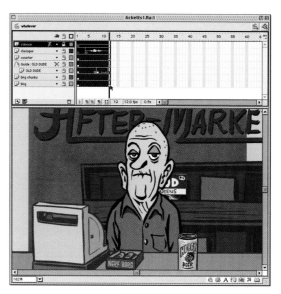

Figure 7.51 Would you give a fake I.D. to this man?

Figure 7.52 Trivia Flash 4 would keep the layer names.

3. The layer that you pasted the frames into will end at the right frame. The other new layers will have extra frames. As in Figure 7.53, select them using the layer you pasted the frames into as a guide for the correct frame to start at, and delete the extra frames (Shift-F5).

Figure 7.53 Toss the unnecessary frames.

It's a good idea to set a row of blank keyframes at the end of the original scene so the chunks won't show up when they're not wanted. You can then move the keyframes from the scene you pasted in onto layers from the original scene to keep the layer count down. If you pasted in a guide or mask layer, there has to be a corresponding Guide or Mask layer in the original scene. Don't move them otherwise.

CAMERA MOVES

Okay, so Flash doesn't have a real movie camera to move around (as in Toon Boom Studio). But that doesn't mean that you can't hum a few bars and fake it. This section explains how to create a number of typical camera moves.

Multiplane

The *Multiplane* technique is derived from a special camera rig that uses multiple levels of artwork. A track allows the camera to plunge through the levels of artwork, creating the sense of three dimensions. (Disney is credited with building the first Multiplane camera.) As you'll see, you can use a bit of trickery in Flash to emulate this effect. A little easing, and even some overshoot can give your camera moves a natural feel, and take some of the computery edge off them.

To simulate parallax shift, just move the layers at different rates. The farther away something is, the less it shifts. Getting the feel right is a matter of trial and error. It's a good idea to try to avoid showing things that need to be firmly planted on the ground (such as feet, trees, lampposts) where they connect with the ground. It's certainly possible to do a multiplane effect when you see these things, but it makes it much more difficult to make it look right. You can try cleverly covering it up with a foreground layer.

In the scene shown in Figures 7.54 and 7.55 (from the file called multiplane.fla on the CD-ROM), the camera move goes left to right, revealing the chicken. The background moves a little bit, and the background tree moves slightly more. But the foreground tree moves a lot more, and it slides along the ground. The rock, which moves the most, drops below frame so the bottom isn't shown. The chicken can do whatever it wants. The problem is that the background is a single piece. The ground does not move in perspective, but here's how you can fake it:

Figure 7.54 What chicken?

Figure 7.55 Ah, that one!

1. Open multiplane.fla, and switch to the exercise scene. Create a new symbol and then place the background bitmap (Bitmap 53) in the symbol with the horizon line at the center point, as shown in Figure 7.56.

2. Make a Mask layer. Draw a rectangle to reveal only the ground up to the horizon line, as shown in Figure 7.57.

Figure 7.56 Look closely, and you'll see the center point.

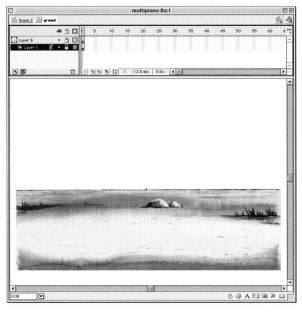

Figure 7.57 Make sure both layers are locked when you're finished.

3. In the main timeline, make a new layer just above the background layer. Copy the first background keyframe and paste it into the new layer to keep the current scaling and position. In the Instance Palette, swap the background you just pasted in with the masked ground symbol, as shown in Figure 7.58.

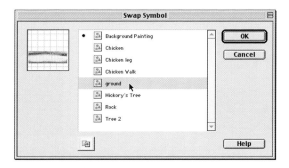

Figure 7.58 Swap Symbol gets the job done.

4. After swapping, adjust the position of the ground symbol to match the background. Using the Rotate tool, grab the bottom middle rotate handle to skew the ground symbol to the left (Figure 7.59).

5. Set a keyframe at the last frame of the ground symbol layer. At this keyframe, skew the ground the other direction. Set a tween.

The horizon is far off enough to not need to move, although you can move it slightly if you want. Moving all these chunks at the same time is processor-intensive, but effective use of multiplane can actually help you get symbols off the Stage sooner than others, and therefore give Flash less to process.

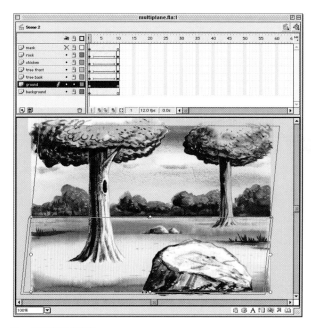

Figure 7.59 Skew slightly.

Figures 7.60 and 7.61 show an example of a tilt shot that uses multiplane to reveal the chicken behind the rock. It works the same way as the horizontal move. The closer the items are to the camera, the more it moves. The fake ground perspective was used, but instead of skewing, the ground was scaled vertically.

Figure 7.60 Where did that chicken go now?

Figure 7.61 He's behind the rock again. Duh.

Figuring out which chunks to move and how much can be difficult. The best way to figure it out is to observe the real world. Fix your eye on a far away spot, and move your body in the direction of the camera move you want to simulate. Turning your head is not sufficient, although that does simulate a pan.

Zooming

A zoom is easily accomplished with some scaling. Scaling tends to be processor-intensive, so use this with few items, or limit the amount of scaling. Open up the zoom.fla file from the CD-ROM and select the zoom exercise scene.

1. Make sure there's a complete column of keyframes because everything will need to move at once. Set another column of keyframes for the end of the zoom, and add tweens to all layers, as shown in Figure 7.62

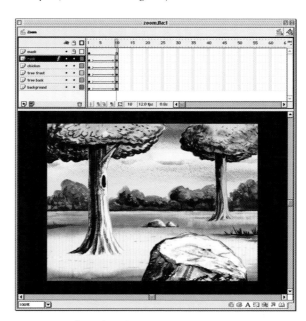

Figure 7.62 Don't forget the easing!

2. Make sure all the layers that you're zooming are unlocked. At the end keyframe, Select All. Now scale everything up or down, depending on whether you're zooming in (Figure 7.63) or out.

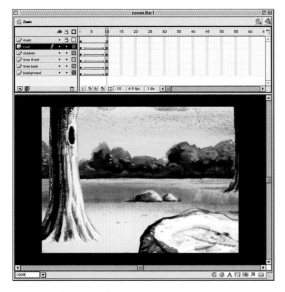

Figure 7.63 A simple zoom in.

Figure 7.64 Looking for chicken in all the wrong places.

You may want to scale the objects using the Transform palette, which scales around the center of all the objects; however, you might want to offset the zoom a bit to focus in on a specific point.

A dolly in or out shot uses scaling like a zoom, but it simulates the camera being on a track and actually moving towards or away from the scene. This means that there's some parallax shift, so it's another multiplane situation. The closer the camera comes to an item, the bigger it gets, but it will also move to the side and eventually off screen if the camera passes it. Suppose we want to dolly in on the same scene (Figure 7.64) to reveal the chicken behind the rock. Open up the dolly exercise scene.

1. Start with a column of keyframes. Set an end column of keyframes and tweens. At the end keyframe, Select All, and scale everything up a bit, as shown in Figure 7.65.

Figure 7.65 This is scaled up 10%.

2. Move the rock down and to the right so that most of it goes off screen. Scale it up, as shown in Figure 7.66. If the rock looks like it's just sliding around when you play the scene, you need to scale it up more, or adjust the position.

Figure 7.66 A little closer and there's that darn chicken.

3. Scale the chicken up a bit and move it down and to the right, but not as much as the rock because it's farther from the camera. You may want to lock off the other layers, as shown in Figure 7.67.

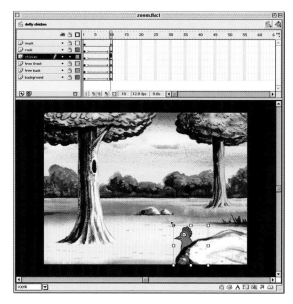

Figure 7.67 A slightly larger chicken.

4. Scale the tree on the left, and move it to the left. Because of the scaling, you may not need to move it down much. Make sure it does not scale more than the rock.

Scale up and move the back tree if you like, but it's far off enough that it isn't necessary. Keep playing it back while you scale, and move the objects to make sure it looks natural. The problem of objects shifting position on the ground can't really be covered up the way it was with the previous examples, so hide the base of the tree or the chicken's feet if you can. Or frame the shot so they don't show at all.

TRANSITIONS

Aside from a cut, there are several ways to go from one scene to another that are easily accomplished in Flash. This section provides the hints you need to create those wonderfully clichéd, er, textbook effects you've come to know and love (or hate). You'll need to use the transition.fla file from the CD-ROM for this section.

Fade to Black

Ah, the old classic, fade to black. It's a cinch! Open up the fade exercise scene.

1. Create a new layer and put it above everything else that appears on Stage. Set a keyframe for the start of the fade at frame 6. Make a black rectangle that covers the Stage. Group it and make it a symbol (Figure 7.68).

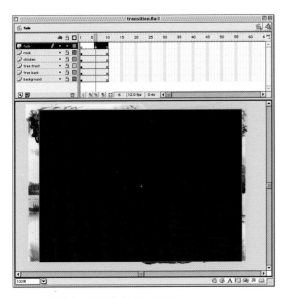

Figure 7.68 No, it's not the obelisk from 2001.

2. Add a keyframe in the last frame for the end of the fade, and set a tween. Go back to the first keyframe of the fade; then select the rectangle. In the Effect palette, change the effect to Alpha, and set the percent to a low number (Figure 7.69).

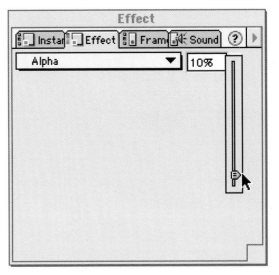

Figure 7.69 Alpha tweening can be processor-intensive, so keep these fades short.

There's no point in setting the Alpha percent to zero because that makes it completely transparent and, therefore, identical to the previous frame. Of course, you can fade to any color, but black is the most common. You can always fade in from black as well.

Iris

An iris opens a porthole view into a scene, or closes a porthole view on the way out of a scene. In either case, it's easy to create an iris effect, with just a handful of steps. Open up the iris exercise scene in the transition.fla file.

1. Create a new layer, and put it above everything else that appears on Stage. At frame 6, set a keyframe for the start of the iris. Make a black rectangle that covers the Stage. Now draw a small circle outside of the rectangle and group it, as shown in Figure 7.70.

2. Center the grouped circle on the rectangle (Figure 7.71). When it's in the right place, break the circle apart and then deselect. Now double-click the circle, and delete it. Group the rectangle with the hole, and make it a symbol. Use the Info palette to center the circle, if you'd like.

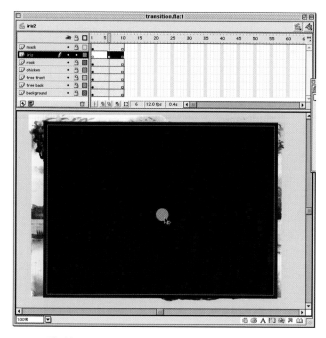

Figure 7.71 The iris at center.

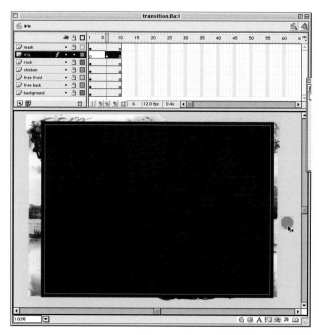

Figure 7.70 The color of the circle doesn't matter.

3. Set a keyframe in the last frame for the end of the iris, and add a tween. Depending on whether you want to iris in or out, select the first keyframe or the last, and scale the iris mask up. The circular hole should just reach the edges of the frame, as shown in Figure 7.72.

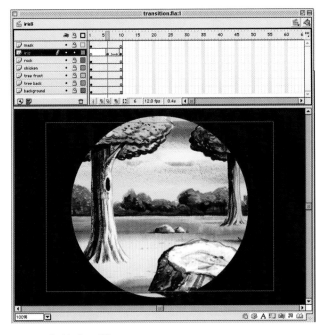

Figure 7.72 An iris view of the scene.

Depending on how small you made the hole, you may have to scale a ridiculous amount. Unfortunately, the info palette will only allow you to scale an item to the width of the pasteboard. If this keeps you from scaling the iris mask big enough, use the Zoom tool to view the Stage as small as possible (8%); then scale the mask past the pasteboard, as shown in Figure 7.73.

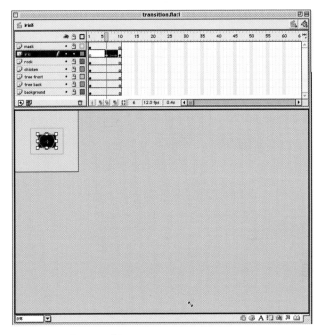

Figure 7.73 Now *that's* a small Stage.

It's a good idea to use some easing when you use an iris transition because the scaling is so excessive. You may also want to put a completely black frame after the end of the iris in, or before the start of the iris out.

Wipes

You can wipe from one scene to the next with an animated mask. It's a good idea to keep the movement in the scenes to a minimum when you're doing the wipe. The transition shown in Figure 7.74, for example, goes from the scene of the chicken coming out from behind the rock to the exterior of Jickett's.

Figure 7.74 A wipe from chickens to hot rods.

Only after the wipe has finished does the Tudor drive on. In this example, just the background of the shop needs to be masked, but if necessary, the car can be a masked layer as well. If it used a Guide layer, however, the entire scene would have to be made into an animated symbol because you can't mask a guided layer. Or you could wipe off the chicken and rock scene instead.

1. Open up the wipe exercise scene. A new layer (jicketts bkg) has been created above the existing scene. The scene you want to wipe to has already been pasted into the layer, as shown in Figure 7.75.

Figure 7.75 Chickens to hot rods?

2. Make a mask layer above the layers that will be wiped. Set those layers to Masked, as shown in Figure 7.76.

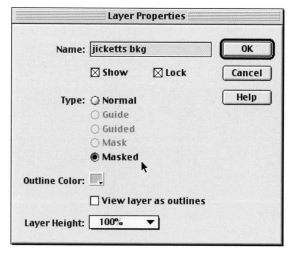

Figure 7.76 Use the Layer Properties dialog box to set the mask.

3. Set a keyframe in the Mask layer at the start of the wipe (frame 6), and put in the symbol (fade) you want to use for the transition. Set a keyframe for the end of the wipe at frame 12, and make sure the mask covers the entire Stage, or is replaced by a symbol that can cover the Stage. Add a tween and then make sure the mask and masked layers are locked, as shown in Figure 7.77.

If the wipe does not begin with the first frame, make sure there's something in the mask layer (probably off the Stage completely) until the wipe begins. Otherwise, Flash gets confused.

Remember that the mask can be any shape (even text!), and can go across the screen from any direction. There are endless possibilities for this technique. Figures 7.78 and 7.79 show a pair of examples. Unfortunately, you can't feather a mask in Flash, so you can't quite get those Kurosawa-style transitions.

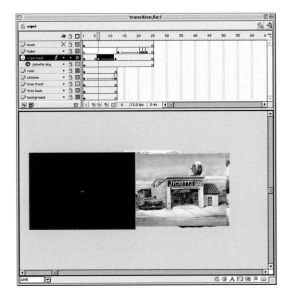

Figure 7.77 Slide that mask!

Figure 7.78 A wipe using a circular mask.

Figure 7.79 Another wacky wipe.

Dissolves

A crossfade, or dissolve, sounds like a good idea, but it's extremely processor-intensive and most often does not provide the desired effect. Any overlapping chunks will go transparent and show the overlap, which is particularly bad if you have any digital puppets on the Stage, as demonstrated by Figure 7.80. If you must use a dissolve, best to fade in only the background, although it is possible to make an entire scene an animated symbol and fade that in. This works exactly like a fade to black, except that you're fading to a background (or whole scene) instead of a black rectangle. Open up the dissolve exercise scene in the transition.fla file.

Figure 7.80 Hideous!

1. A new layer (jicketts bkg) has been added above the existing scene. Set a keyframe at frame 8 for the start of the dissolve, and place the background symbol (jicketts bkg) into it, as shown in Figure 7.81.

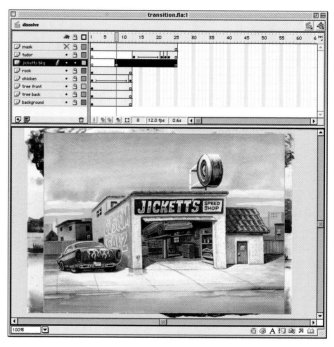

Figure 7.81 Make sure the background is a symbol.

2. Set another keyframe at frame 12 for the end of the dissolve, and add a tween (Figure 7.82). Select the background at the first keyframe, and in the effects palette, set the alpha to a low percentage.

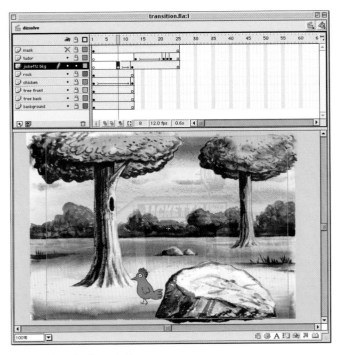

Figure 7.82 About five frames is plenty.

It's important to keep the dissolve short. Try to have as few moving things as possible on screen during the dissolve. In the sample file, the chicken walks during the dissolve so you can see how much an alpha tween slows things down.

FADE TO NEXT CHAPTER

Use the cinematic approach shown here and you'll begin to think of your Flash movies *more as movies*, and less as internet thingies. Plan those scenes carefully, consider the camera moves, nail those transitions, and you'll be primed for that awards gala. (But not before you consider the soundtrack, the sound effects, and the dialogue—which are covered in the next chapter.)

8

Sound—
Half the Experience

The final ingredient you need to add to your animation is sound. Sound has been described as being "half the experience" of any animation, so obviously this is a crucial element. Great animation is great with or without sound, but good sound design really makes the action come alive. The addition of sound takes away the last layer of abstraction from your animation. To the audience, it makes the experience of watching animation immediate and direct instead of an interpretation.

It's a good test of quality animation to watch with the sound turned off. Notice how much easier it is to concentrate on the character animation itself—the technique—without sound. But then try listening to just the sound without visuals. The music, dialogue, and sound effects should also tell a story, preferably the same one you watched with the sound off. The story may not be as clearly told or as obvious, but the music will provide emotional ups and downs, the dialogue will add expression, and the sound effects will add punctuation.

THE TRUTH ABOUT STREAMING SOUND

If sound is half the experience of animation, in Flash it's at least half the download time. If you use any streaming sound, you've pretty much committed yourself to using streaming sound throughout the entire movie. Streaming sound forces Flash to maintain the frame rate at the cost of skipping frames when necessary. Without streaming sound, the frame rate drops when the animation gets too complicated for the computer's processor. If you have intermittent streaming sound, the frame rate will probably be different when there's streaming sound and when there isn't. There will also be the tendency to skip frames after the streaming sound has stopped.

Music loops, single words, short sound effects (like footsteps), and long sound effects that need to only "hit" once (like explosions) can be added to your animations as Event sounds. Like anything else in the library, Event sounds can be used multiple times but only need to be loaded once, which makes music loops particularly efficient, albeit repetitive. The Peculia cartoon (which you can find on richardsala.com and on the CD) uses only Event sound,

but there is no dialogue. There are two music loops and a couple of stings; however, making the eerie music box tune fade out was guesswork based on the assumption that the movie would play back at 12 fps, more or less.

For more ambitious or accurate sound design, streaming sound is the only way to go. You must use it all the way through your movie (even when there is silence) to maintain the frame rate. Flash's MP3 compression uses a constant bit rate (determined in the Publish menu), so in terms of file size, it makes no difference if you have lots of sounds going on or near silence. It only matters how long streaming sound is being used. That being the case, you might as well use sound whenever you can.

TIP All Streaming sounds get the same compression, and all Event sounds get the same compression unless otherwise specified. If you have Event sounds in your movie, use the lowest acceptable bit rate for compression, and if need be, set a higher bit rate for individual sounds. In the David Boring trailer (which can also be found on the CD or www.pantheonbooks.com), the gunshot sound is set to a lower compression higher bit rate setting than everything else because at the default compression, it sounded too muffled.

RECORDING

Unless you absolutely don't care about file size (that is, you're aiming for video), your sound is going to be compressed, probably quite a bit. It's true that the better the sound quality going in, the better it compresses, and the better it sounds coming out. However, if you're going to be exporting your .swf with 24 kbps MP3 compression, in all honesty you can often get away with some fairly low-quality sound recording. You don't have to rent time in a professional sound studio—the d-i-y approach can suffice.

This is by no means a license to do so, but an inexpensive microphone (although not the junk that comes with most sound cards) and low noise levels are just about all you need for typical Flash audio quality. Unless you strongly suspect you'll be showing your Flash animation on television someday, your cartoon won't benefit much from booking studio time. Better to spend your money on quality performers than quality equipment.

SOUND EDITING 101

Flash offers basic control over sound. You can choose when a sound starts and stops, the in and out points of the sound itself, how many times a sound loops, and you can adjust the envelope (volume levels). That's about it. Fortunately, you really don't need a whole lot more than that. There are a few functions that Flash won't do, though, and for them you'll need to turn to a sound editing program. On the PC side, Sonic Foundry's Sound Forge (www.sonicfoundry.com) gets the job done with aplomb. On the Mac side, you can't go wrong with Bias Peak (www.bias-inc.com). Both programs come in full and "lite" versions to suit your budget.

Flash can't turn up the volume. It is at its highest by default, and you can only lower it from there. If you have an audio clip that isn't loud enough, you can either turn down the volume of all your other sounds, or you can adjust the gain in a sound editing program.

TIP When you normalize a file in a sound editor, you essentially set the volume to a certain level to be able to maximize the file's dynamic range.

In this corner... Mooney's brilliant plan for putting out a fire.

When in doubt, normalize everything and then lower the individual volume of the sound clips in Flash. Record everything at least at 22kHz, 16 bit, but don't bother with stereo. (You may want to record at 44kHz, put away the original recording for safekeeping, and then convert down to suit.) Stick with mono sound. Plenty of people have their left and right speakers mixed up, or not far enough apart to make any difference. In fact, plenty of people don't even have sound cards in their computers (amazing, huh?).

Legend has it that Brian Wilson, the genius behind the Beach Boys, would listen to the band's recordings on a single crummy speaker to make sure that the songs would sound good on a car radio. You should apply that same wisdom to the world of Flash cartooning. No matter how good your cartoon sounds on a killer set of speakers, it had better sound great on a tinny internal PC speaker, too. Test the sound of your toons on a variety of speaker setups, and you'll deliver justice to all.

DIALOGUE

Editing dialogue involves two things: picking the best take, and adjusting the timing. Assuming you have more than one take from which to choose, picking the best take of a particular line of dialogue isn't always as easy as it seems. The dialogue has to be easily understood by a first time listener, exemplify the character at the particular moment the dialogue is being spoken and still be within character, and if necessary, be funny.

This difficulty can be greatly compounded if the dialogue is part of an exchange between characters that were recorded at different times. The dialogue must flow together naturally to make it seem as though the characters are really talking *to* each other rather than *at* each other. Even a shouting match has a natural flow to it.

Sometimes the best method is simply trial and error. On a line-by-line basis, cut out the best takes, or the most varied, and save them using a sequential naming convention, such as [number of scene]-[abbreviated character name]-[a few words describing the line][take number]. Put them into your scene; then mix and match until you find the combination that flows best, or has the best rhythm. Make sure you remove the unused takes when you're done, or your Flash file will be unnecessarily large.

Setting the Timing

Adjusting the timing of dialogue usually means making it go faster. Dialogue can really eat up screen time, and there are few greater challenges than making a scene of two characters sitting around talking interesting. If you can't cut out whole lines, you'll have to cut down the pauses between lines and words. The key is to do this without making it seem unnatural. Trim pauses between lines before you trim pauses between words. Always do so in tiny increments, playing the whole phrase back constantly. Be aware of where the actor speaking the line should breathe. If you remove a line, or cut in a new one, too short a pause in between makes changes in pitch more obvious (like a bad radio commercial). Some sound editors provide the ability to automatically trim out silent areas from a track, and can also speed up or slow down the track, while maintaining pitch.

When cutting out lines of dialogue to be placed into Flash, it's a good idea to leave a tiny bit of space before the first word. That way, you can adjust the timing within a fraction of a keyframe by changing the in point for the sound.

Dealing with Noise

If you're stuck with a noisy recording or distractions, such as lip licking and tongue clicking, fade out the noise in the pauses. Look at the waveform. If, during the pauses, you see anything but a thin line, you'll hear it, too. Select the area after the end of the word (be careful with words that end in "s") and shortly before the next word, and use your sound editing program's fade out function. If it doesn't have one, adjust the gain in the furthest negative direction, but be aware that this may cause words to "fall off." Music will definitely help cover for poorly recorded dialogue.

NOTE *Gain* is used to boost (raise) or cut (lower) specific frequency bands in a recording.

If your sound editing program has reverb, a little bit never hurt a line of dialogue. Keep it minimal and appropriate to the environment the character is in. Also, MP3 compression tends to flatten out range and make sounds muddy. You may want to adjust the equalization of your dialogue to add some high end, particularly if the actor has a low-pitched voice or a nasal tone.

NOTE *Reverb* (short for reverberation) adds echo to a recording. Different *reverb* settings can simulate different environments, allowing you to create effects ranging from a concert hall to a city sewer. The process of *equalization (EQ)* evens out a sound file, by raising or lowering frequency bands.

MUSIC

Music is another key ingredient in sound design, and can define the style of an animation almost as well as the drawing does. Take an animation and watch it with *The Merry-Go-Round Broke Down*; then watch it with some techno-blather, and you'll find that you've watched two totally different cartoons.

The problem with good music is that it's hard to come by. If you can find someone to compose, orchestrate, and record a score for your cartoon, fantastic. But failing that, you'll have to find something and then make it fit. Licensing even obscure music can be expensive, and the usage rights for Internet properties are still a tricky area. Read the fine print carefully on those inexpensive CDs that claim to be "royalty-free." More often than not, it means "royalty-free for use on your answering machine." Genuinely royalty-free music does exist, but it tends to be fairly expensive, or only comes in short, loopable chunks.

Getting some musician buddies of yours to record an original composition for you is a good way to ensure that the rights aren't a problem, but make sure that all parties sign an agreement to that effect. Everyone knows someone who's in a band, but keep in mind that musicianship varies just as much as acting ability.

Toon Tunes

NPR's The Connection has an archived show on their website called *Toon Tunes* (August 23, 2001), which is about cartoon music with a focus on the great Carl Stalling. The show also features interviews with Shirley Walker *(Batman, Superman),* and Mark Mothersbaugh *(Rugrats, Pee-Wee's Playhouse).* Check it out at www.theconnection.org/archive/2001/08/0823b.shtml.

SOUND EFFECTS

An interesting point about sound effects is that the actual sound does not in any way have to correspond with the element supposedly making the sound in your cartoon. Just because your character drops a can filled with nuts and bolts doesn't mean you need a sound effect of a can filled with nuts and bolts. What you need is something that suggests and punctuates that action. Only the eagle-eared and the person who picked the sound effects will know for sure what the sound really is, but that doesn't matter. All that matters is that the sound effect work in conjunction with the action.

What sound comes to mind when someone gets punched? A real punch at most sounds like a dull thud (kids—don't try this at home). But a cartoon (or kung fu movie) punch is usually a high-pitched snapping noise. Using a realistic sound can actually be detrimental to your cartoon because, like the animation itself, it's all about exaggeration and artistic interpretation. An unexpected or incongruous sound effect can make a funny moment out of something that isn't especially funny. Also, there are specific sounds forever linked to certain cartoon actions, and by using familiar sounds you help sell the action.

Like royalty-free music CDs, read the fine print to make sure sound effects CDs are royalty-free for use in your cartoon. At Twinkle, we favor the *A Poke in the Ear with a Sharp Stick* series from Rarefaction (www.rarefaction.com), particularly volume two. They're extremely high quality recordings of very unusual sounds.

Not every action requires a sound effect—just the ones that need emphasis. If the primary action is of the character walking, footstep sound effects are a good idea. But if the primary action is of the character chewing gum while walking, gum-chewing sound effects are a good idea, and footsteps probably aren't necessary. Just as in presenting actions, sound effects should go one at a time. Does this mean that if your character is flying a plane and firing a machine gun that there should only be sound effects for the plane's engine or the machine gun, but not both? Of course not. But in this case, the engine qualifies as ambient sound (background noise), while the machine gun needs sound effects. If you've got Squeaky the Dog and Jingles the Cat onscreen at the same time, of course you give them both sound effects. Just emphasize the one performing the primary action.

MIXING

Because there's no way to know what kind of computer your animation will be seen (and heard) on, make sure your sound mix is listenable on a built-in computer speaker. (Thank you, Brian Wilson.) Keep other levels low during dialogue. Be aware of the overall volume of your cartoon. Try comparing it to the volume of your system alert noise. If you have to crank up the overall volume of your computer to hear your cartoon, you might want to raise the gain on your sound files—but make sure they don't clip.

> **NOTE** Clipping is a distortion that happens when a sound's amplitude exceeds the maximum recording level. A clipped track sounds as if it's been "cut off."

As tempting as it may be, don't pre-mix your sound. Instead, assemble your tracks in Flash. Although it takes more effort to adjust sound levels in Flash, it's much easier to adjust the timing this way. In the end, good timing is far more important than good sound.

> **TIP** Sometimes, certain sounds will "peak" and have a crackling, distorted sound even though the waveform is not at all clipped. If this happens, lower the levels slightly for that particular sound and re-export.

QUIET ON THE SET!

Sound can help make a great cartoon, just as soon as it can break it. The next chapter explains how sound was incorporated into the first episode of *Jickett's Speed Shop*—from the soundtrack, through the dialogue and special effects. Opening with an interview, the chapter moves into a scene-by-scene dissection of the cartoon.

9

Makin' the Show— Jickett's Speed Shop

Jickett's *Speed Shop* began as a short comic book story called *Tired*. Written and drawn by Doug Allen, the first part originally ran in Issue 23 of the Fantagraphics anthology, *Zero Zero*. The second part was conceived of but never completed. When Twinkle began developing properties, *Tired* was a natural.

To get into the meat and potatoes of the making of *Jickett's Speed Shop*, this chapter takes a different format from the rest of the book. We pop into interview mode to dig out the gory details and then look at the first episode of *Jickett's*, frame-by-frame.

WRITING THE EPISODE

Dan G: Turning Tired *into* Jickett's Speed Shop *must have been quite an experience. How did the writing process start out?*

John K: Using the comic book story as a launching point, the three of us (Doug, Gary, and I) locked ourselves in a room and figured out what happens after the existing material ends. We had the beginning of a story, and characters.

Dan G: It seems like the characters would have to come first. What was involved in the character development process?

John K: We fleshed out the characters by coming up with short biographies for each of them. Whether or not these details specifically get revealed in any of the episodes is not the point. When working on the show, we need to know who these characters are so that the things they do and say are grounded in the show's reality. There's no way to know if something is out of character if that character has never been established.

For example, we decided that Ford is about nineteen years old, and has just moved into town. He lives with his parents, loves his car, but is not an especially good mechanic. For all his posturing as a racer, he is at heart a customizer, not a rodder, meaning that he's more interested in his car's appearance than its speed and handling. But there's no scene in the pilot where Ford walks up to Angel and says, "Hey baby, I'm nineteen years old and I just moved into town. Yeah, so what if I live with my parents, but I got me a Tudor and I'm a whiz with a wrench. Honest."

Jicketts and Mooney are the comedy duo, and the bulk of the cartoon hi-jinx would fall on their shoulders. We knew that any time the story started getting too serious, we could always go to Jickett's and lighten things up with some good old-fashioned cartoon violence. In designing the characters, we made Jicketts really huge and Mooney really tiny, while all the others are reasonably humanoid. Because they're so cartoony, they can do anything without stretching credibility.

Dan G: How did the plot develop?

John K: Figuring out the basic story for the pilot was easy, since we knew it would be straight out of *Tired*. We did, however, have to figure out what would happen in the following episodes. Doug had thought out the conclusion of *Tired*, but it soon exploded into a crazed story of hot rods and undead broads. Without revealing the master plan, we can say that Gary's fascination with monsters led to the mysterious Angel causing car crashes to provide body parts for Ed "Big Daddy" Roth-style demons. Why does Angel do this? What do the demons do with the chunks? What is the exact nature of the relationship between Jicketts and Mooney? Will Ford ever get the girl? It's all in the works.

Dan G: *Why did the series title change from the original story?*

John K: We decided that *Tired* wasn't a name that would get anyone very excited, so we chose *Jickett's Speed Shop*, since that would be the main hangout for everyone. It did lead to some confusion, because the character's name is Jicketts, but the shop is called "Jickett's," which would imply that his name is Jickett. So the shop should be called "Jicketts'" or "Jicketts's," but we figured that Jicketts wasn't too big on grammatical correctness.

Dan G: *Did you write an actual script to pitch the series?*

John K: To make the show easier to pitch, we wrote up a script that basically just spelled out what was in *Tired*. It was decided that the pilot episode should be a self-contained story that ended in a cliffhanger, and we added an action-packed race to start off the story that would hint at the weird things to come. However, we never took the script seriously because we knew that we'd write the story with storyboards.

STORYBOARDING

Dan G: *From what I've heard, the storyboarding process was more intense than the initial writing sessions. What went down?*

John K: I ran around the room like a wild man acting out the scenes, followed by my scribbling tiny, inscrutable drawings that outlined the shots. Then, Doug made these nice, drawing them on index cards that worked out the composition. We tacked these cards to the wall to make sure that they made sense and the actions were clear, with a bare minimum of dialogue. If something didn't work, we tried shuffling the cards, or added new ones. But sometimes, we'd have to scrap a whole sequence.

Dan G: *So whole scenes ended up on the proverbial cutting room floor?*

John K: Yes, indeed. For example, we had a great gag where Mooney accidentally burned the post of the lift, and Jicketts whisks him out of the way to yell at him, inadvertently saving him from the falling car. At that point, Mooney sets the phone on fire. However, Jicketts was yelling at Mooney because of what he said about Angel, and we decided that Jicketts would really only care about cars and be indifferent to Angel. So we had to figure out a new way to set the phone on fire.

Also, we storyboarded a sequence introducing another character, Moto—since this was how *Tired* began. But comic books are not cartoons, and the two follow different rules. So we had to adapt *Tired* and be faithful to the tone without slavishly following it. Given the role that Moto plays, it was misleading to put him up front, especially since we presented him in a heroic light. Ford is the protagonist, and the important thing was to establish his character. We would save Moto for later, and with the help of Daniel Clowes we came up with the convenience store scene. This scene establishes what kind of a guy Ford is, gains audience sympathy for him by embarrassing him, and sets up his dramatic need when he sees Angel.

In this corner...Jicketts and Mooney hijinx (hilarity ensues).

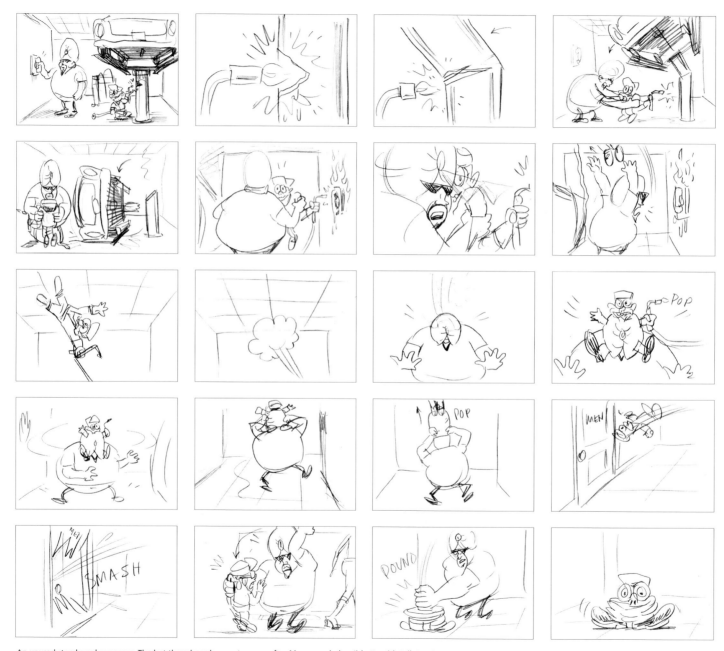

An unused storyboard sequence. The last three boards were to occur after Mooney splashes Jicketts with toilet water.

Dan G: Jicketts isn't just a romantic comedy about car freaks, it's a horror story, too. How did the horror-angle rear its ugly head?

John K: We knew that by horror movie convention, you would never see the monster up front, but you would get an action-packed or suspenseful teaser with a little hint of gore. The key was to find an image that was sufficiently horrifying and intriguing. Eventually we hit upon the severed head in the undamaged car. Harder still was figuring out what would scare Angel, an excellent driver, enough to make her panic and drive the Greaser off the road. We had lots of things that were sufficiently strange, but none of them seemed to directly make her turn the wheel. We knew the image would have something to do with "demonic Angel," but weren't sure what exactly. Then I remembered once having the crap scared out of me when a bird hit my windshield, and the head in the pizza box was the result.

Dan G: The burning phone scene is sheer comedic genius. More than that, it moves the story along like opening up the second and third carburetors on a tri-power manifold. Can you lend some insight on that scene?

John K: For a long time in the storyboards, Ford was not at Jickett's until after the phone fire had been put out and Angel left the shop. But as the protagonist, Ford must be active, so we had him go to Jickett's and try to get Jicketts to call Pizza Stop. Then we had to take him out of the action, because Ford is level-headed enough to be able to put out a small fire. But his Achilles' heel is his car, and the little glob of melted plastic both advanced the plot and illuminated character. It takes Ford out of the action, and it shows what a nut Ford is that he would freak out over such a small thing.

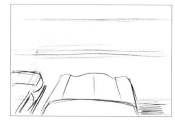

CREATING THE ANIMATIC

Dan G: So once you had your storyboards down, you launched into the animatic. What was that process like?

John K: The animatic was created in Final Cut Pro. We scanned the storyboards and all the panels from *Tired*, Gary did the voices, and we used a demo version of the Jickett's theme by The Mercury Four. The final show had to be four minutes in length, and the first rough cut was about six minutes long, so clearly some editing was required, and nearly all of it was dialogue.

Dan G: Speaking of dialogue, what's the deal with Jicketts' ramble in the opening scene?

John K: When we were first developing Jicketts' character, we decided he would occasionally launch into spacey beat poetry. We wrote a rambling, nonsensical "poem" that Jicketts would recite while the opening race took place, and about half of it eventually got cut out. It was continually argued that the poem should relate to the race in progress and presage the events to occur, but we felt that would make Jicketts too intelligent. Also, Jicketts has no particular supernatural powers. Besides, nothing he could say would make any sense until you saw several more episodes anyway, and we hate that self-referential nudge nudge wink wink stuff.

Dan G: Once the initial scene runs, the flaming Jicketts' logo appears and bam, we're into the scene at the AfterMarket. How did you get things to snap along so smoothly?

John K: The exchange between Ford and the old man at the convenience store was pared down to only the essential insults. By cutting out dialogue, we needed fewer angles of the characters. When the exchange was longer, it was difficult to sustain visual interest in two characters standing around talking, so we had the shot of the old man behind the counter, the shot of Ford, and a master of the two of them from the side. Getting rid of some dialogue made the master shot unnecessary, because there was enough business with the magazine and Ford's fake ID to keep the sequence going. While this whole scene might appear to break the rule of telling the story in pictures and always giving the characters something to do, the previous sequence was the action-packed race, and pacing demanded that the following scene be a slow one. This allows the audience to breathe and also get their bearings, which is important because the race doesn't establish the locations where the rest of the cartoon takes place.

Dan G: Things continue to move at a snappy pace in the next scene, too. Did anything end up on the cutting room floor?

John K: When Ford gets to Jickett's, we again trimmed out some dialogue where Jicketts insults Ford and the quality of Pizza Stop's pizza. It was funny stuff, but we needed to get the action going. The next problem was getting the timing of the action right. The business of Mooney dialing the phone is funny, but it means that Mooney makes the world's fastest phone-in pizza order. Of course we opted for funny over realistic. We kept some of the dialogue by adding more business for Mooney to do while Jicketts talks, but it also led to an amusing way for Mooney to set the phone on fire.

Once the phone is on fire and Angel arrives, we used quite a few panels from *Tired* in the animatic, since we planned to use the same action. One of the things that worked fine in comic form, but not so well in the animatic was the way Mooney ends up splashing Jicketts with the toilet water. The idea of a "toilet-cam" seemed funny to us, and let us sidestep the problem of what exactly causes Mooney to splash Jicketts. Later, we hit upon the idea of Mooney slipping on the Creeper, but we didn't bother putting it in the animatic.

Dan G: And then there's the race …

John K: The race between Ford and Angel is also not very tightly storyboarded because we planned to reuse the symbols of Angel's Gremlin from the opening race. This would dictate the angles we could use, so we again used panels from *Tired* as placeholders. The dialogue between Ford and Angel is another "two people sitting around talking" scene, so again we cut out as much dialogue as possible. The business of the lighter is the excuse for why they're not doing anything. We originally had a callback of Ford's shift knob obsession from the introduction of Moto, but when that scene went, the shift knob thing had to go too. So now the focus of the scene is on Ford's reactions while being suckered into a race, and is another breather before the final burst of action.

RECORDING DIALOGUE

Dan G: The dialogue in Jicketts' Speed Shop *is more akin to cinema than to cartoons. Did you break down and turn the storyboards into a script?*

John K: Absolutely. Once we were sure of the dialogue we wanted to use, we wrote it up in script form. We knew Jicketts' poem would be too long, but we figured we could edit it down later and pick and choose from the best takes. Also, we wanted to allow for improvisation.

Dan G: It sounds like real actors were used for the voices, no?

John K: For the voices of Jicketts and Ford, we hired Torben Brooks, a professional voiceover actor and relative of Gary Leib. Torben really captured the naïve, well-intentioned quality we wanted Ford to have, and made him very sympathetic. He also played Ford completely straight, as opposed to broad and cartoony (except when he had to freak out about the car).

It took a few tries to get Jicketts' voice right. Sometimes you have an actor in mind who has the kind of voice you're looking for, but sometimes you just have to wait until you hear it. Torben made up this wacky accent, and really got the spacey insanity as well as the anger. You just never know what's going to pop out of Jicketts' mouth at any given moment. When he turned "Merv Griffin" into a question, we almost ruined the take by laughing out loud. One tip about casting voices is to pick actors who physically resemble the characters they portray. Torben is by no means fat, but he's a big dude, and he can sound like a really fat guy. But he can also pull off a skinny kid, too. Apparently, Gert Fröbe spoke gibberish while filming *Goldfinger*, and they later dubbed in his voice using an actor who was about his size. No one ever notices it's not him saying, "No Mr. Bond, I expect you to die!"

We had worked with Tess Gill on the *Beef Baron* pilot, and we knew she'd be perfect for Angel. We also kind of wanted to make up for making her play a pig in *Beef Baron*. She can do a sweet, sexy voice but isn't afraid to try anything. Plus, she has a great scream that we unfortunately never got to use. She really gave lots of different colorings to the lines that we could choose from, and each one implied something different. Angel has to be matter-of-fact, flirtatious, playful, and downright dangerous all at the same time or within a beat, and Tess nailed it.

PICKING UP THE CHUNKS

Dan G: So you had the storyboards, you had the dialogue, and you had the animatic. What was the next step?

John K: Once the animatic was as tight as possible, we had to find the best way to present the actions. We figured out what backgrounds would be needed to accommodate the angles we planned to use. Since most of the backgrounds would be painted, we tried to make each one useful for multiple shots. For many shots, particularly close-ups and inserts, we used a generic watercolor texture background. This helped to keep the focus on the action, and eliminated the need for a new background.

Dan G: Conserving bandwidth is always a consideration with Flash cartoons. What other methods were used to keep the file size down?

John K: We tried to keep the number of car angles to a minimum and still have enough for dynamic racing sequences. This was particularly true of the Trans Am, since it is unlikely that it will ever be featured prominently in another episode of *Jickett's*.

Based on the animatic, we decided what angles and poses of each character would be needed to make the show. There's only one drawing of the old man, because part of the humor of his character is that he's completely deadpan. But there are fifteen different Mooneys, nine replacement heads, and ten different replacement arms because he has to perform so many actions.

Doug drew all the pieces in a two-day pencilling marathon and then went back to his area in upstate New York to ink. As he finished chunks, he scanned, Streamlined, and emailed them to Twinkle, and I started animating.

JICKETT'S SHOT BY SHOT

Ready for the ultimate cartoon dissection? It's time to tear apart the first episode of *Jicketts Speed Shop* shot-by-shot. You can see each of the scenes here in print. John's commentary provides an authoritative and detailed look into one of the most fantastic Flash cartoons ever made. And to top it off, the CD-ROM features a special version of the episode (Jicketts-controller.swf) with an ultra-cool DVD-like controller that allows you to move through the animation frame-by-frame. (From left to right, the navigation buttons provide the following functions: jump back, move back one frame, stop, play, move forward one frame, jump forward.)

Shot 1 It took Tess a while to nail the opening line, but she really got it once we told her it was the equivalent of saying "Gentlemen, start your engines." Fade from black.

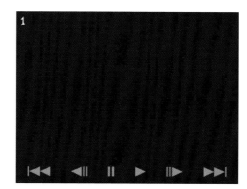

Shot 2 We wanted to start the show with the race already in progress (start late, end early). Squishing the cricket is a cheap gag, but at least it's Angel who's doing the squishing. Insects aren't particularly cute, but the twitching of the antennae helps. You'll be seeing this background many times throughout the show. Using an alpha tween to fade in or out of a scene is very

processor-intensive, so keep the tweens short. The cricket does not come on until after the tween is done.

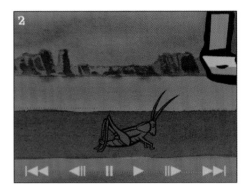

Shot 3 There aren't many "camera moves" in the pilot, but this is one of them. We tended to avoid them because they're usually processor intensive, but we wanted a lot of movement in the race to keep the energy level up. Originally, this shot was going to start on the tire to tie it to the previous shot, but it wasn't necessary and tended to point out the lack of perspective change. The headlight glow is a simple radial gradient of white to white with an alpha of 0%. The background is the first use of the generic watercolor blob.

Shot 4 Here's the same background from shot 2, only it's looping behind them. This is the introduction to the Greaser in the Trans Am, and we wanted to establish that he was having trouble keeping up with Angel. This side-by-side shot is easy to do, and we had to resist using it too often.

Shot 5 There's a substantial amount of easing from the far-away keyframe to foreground. Otherwise, the cars covered the distance too quickly. Although there's no way the Greaser could be that far behind the Gremlin, given where we show him in the shots before and after, we wanted to make it clear where he was. One action at a time!

Shot 6 The Greaser goes fender to fender. Okay, so we did use that shot one more time.

Shot 7 A simple head-swap makes the Greaser look Angel's way. This is a potentially confusing shot because the Greaser appears to be going the opposite direction, but it didn't seem too jarring in the animatic.

Shot 8 The reverse angle shows Angel blowing him a kiss. The heart is a wacky cartoon-ism, but without it, it was unclear exactly what she was doing.

Shot 9 It was tricky jointing Angel's boot at the ankle, but otherwise the shin would have moved too much, and the whole thing would look wrong. Note the overshoot to show that Angel really put the pedal to the metal. We actually failed to do the research and were unsure what Gremlin pedals looked like, but this gets the idea across. There's that watercolor blob again.

Shot 10 The cutaway piston shot was meant to establish that something weird was creeping into Angel's car, but now it just shows some inner workings. In watching a lot of racing movies, there are always cuts to close-ups of the machines.

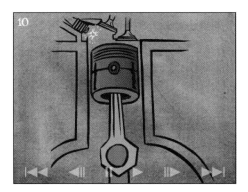

Shot 11 This shot of Angel outstripping the Greaser uses the same background as shot 5, but with a movie clip of the stripes and animated signs to give the illusion of speed.

Shot 12 Sometimes a blink and a good moronic stare are all you need.

Shot 13 This shot is physically impossible, but you can get away with that kind of stuff in cartoons. The fist is large enough to cover the arm, so it wasn't necessary to animate any of the Greaser's body. The stick itself is the same in each position, just turned upside-down and scaled for the shift. A little overshoot sells the action.

Shot 14 Having both cars in the frame establishes the physical relationship, but the problem here is that if the Gremlin got too close, the perspective was obviously wrong. Rather than make Doug draw another angle of the Gremlin that might only get used once, we pushed the limit of believability and then cut away. The spinning rims are enough to give the Trans Am the illusion of movement. Since the camera is theoretically locked to the bumper, the car must stay in the same place while everything else moves around it.

Shot 15 Here's the first use of this angle. The vanishing point is offscreen, so we could cheat the perspective a little. If the Gremlin and Trans Am were side-by-side, you'd notice that the perspectives don't quite match for this angle. Quick cutting really helps cover up that sort of thing, and also makes the race feel faster.

Shot 16 This shot had to move quickly because it was obviously a zoom in on a single piece with no perspective shift. This is the same drawing of the Greaser that's in the previous shot, and his shoulder seems a little odd, but it goes by so fast it doesn't matter.

Shot 17 This is the same car used in shot 3, but the camera move is slightly different. After the previous shot, this zoom in had to start closer to keep up the pacing. Also, the background is a wacky green to hint that things are about to go wrong.

Shot 18 This shot of the piston was supposed to have green goop in it, or a mysterious glow of some kind, but it never looked right so we simply made the piston go faster and left it at that.

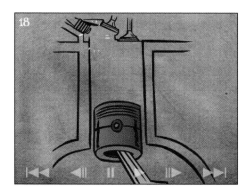

Shot 19 This was another potential cause of confusion since we hadn't previously established what Angel's shift knob looked like. However, we trusted that the previous cuts would indicate that we were in Angel's car. We've shown the Greaser's shift knob, so who else could this be?

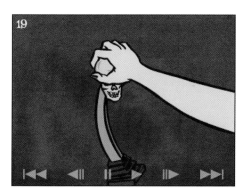

Shot 20 Some simple facial animation here. We wanted to build some suspense by cutting away to Angel's reaction instead of immediately showing the goop on her hand. We also wanted to show that Angel doesn't spook easily.

Shot 21 The goop is doing a little squash and stretch with the center point where it's attached to the skull. The arm pivots at the elbow as it should, with some overshoot.

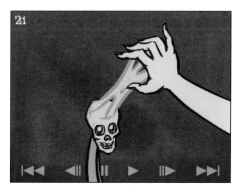

Shot 22 Here's the same angle used in shot 15. This seemed to be the best way to show the Trans Am getting ahead of the Gremlin, but the shot had to go by quickly because of the perspective cheat.

Shot 23 Another camera move, this time up the hood of the Trans-Am. In the storyboards, the Greaser is grinning here because he's finally winning, but the shot goes by fast enough that it didn't merit drawing a new head.

Shot 24 Angel takes her eyes off the road to look at the goop on her hand. We've never seen her from this angle before, but this jarring moment helps point out that something is wrong.

Shot 25 In a horror movie, what's suggested is always scarier than what's actually seen. Roger Corman's theory was that the scariest thing is a closed door. This is why the pizza box flies at the car for so long in a sequence otherwise made of quick cuts. We needed an image that was sufficiently strange to cause Angel to swerve wildly. Angel doesn't move much in this shot, but the focus should be on the box. The pizza box is on a single motion path and rotates without changing perspective until it opens up. The head hits the windshield quickly and then we cut away so you don't get a good look at it, as per horror movie convention.

Shot 26 Angel's right arm does some wacky things in this shot, but it goes by quickly. Although the action is very quick, we had to keep her on screen long enough for it to register, so we actually cut later than originally planned. The background changes to red to amplify her fear.

Shot 27 Flash isn't too good at dealing with perspective shifts, so this overhead shot was the only way to clearly indicate what happens.

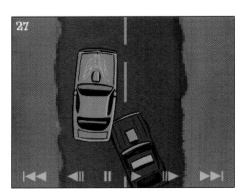

Shot 28 This shot alone would not be enough to sell the accident because it goes by too quickly. But the action is already established by the previous shot, and this is just another angle of the same action. Note that there's actually no damage to either car. How fortunate!

Shot 29 The Trans Am's pivot point is at the front axle so it would slide reasonably. It was actually much harder to get the angle of the Gremlin to look right. The skid marks are uncovered using an animated mask.

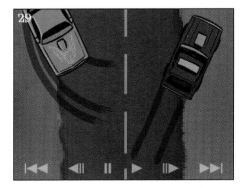

Shot 30 This is the only serious "camera move" of the entire show. The angle of the car is a little odd for the first few frames, but it's only a few frames. The car covers over the hole that's already in the barrier. The road chunk is a .png file with an alpha channel. There's a little multiplane for the reveal of the undamaged car. In the original camera move, the shot continued and zoomed in on the car, but it was too processor intensive. The car was supposed to be smoking, but that, in combination with the camera move, slowed down even the fastest computers.

Shot 31 If you look closely, you'll see that there's only a drawing of half the interior, but it's duplicated and flopped horizontally. The interior is masked off by the foreground car. The head is onscreen just long enough to make you wonder what happened to his body.

Shot 32 Then we immediately move on to some funny stuff. We originally had the previous shot fade out of Jicketts' sunglasses, but it was funnier to start on his fat belly. The image of him sitting in the car came out of the storyboards. I guess we might have written "Jicketts finishes his poem, and we pull out to reveal that he's sitting in the engine compartment of a car in his approximation of the lotus position" but it's unlikely. The really funny stuff comes from images.

Shot 33 The hood slamming on Jicketts is definitely a case of fast is funny. It's really got to slam on his head, but you have to see it coming. Mooney bounces in, knocks the bar, the hood bounces up, and then slams down. One action at a time. The talking turban is pure squash and stretch.

Shot 34 The flames in the Jickett's logo are three replacement shapes. The gradient in them varies in position to give them a flickering look.

Shot 35 This was the first shot to be animated. This whole sequence owes more than a little to *Raising Arizona*. (Steal from the best!). This is a very simple action, but the little things help sell it. The can bounces a bit, and the index finger lets go of the can before the hand lifts off. The finger was animated within the hand symbol to keep it in place.

Shot 36 The background is the good ol' watercolor blob again. We found that it worked best to not have any black lines on background items. Otherwise, the characters did not stand out enough, particularly the old man, who doesn't move much. Getting the arm to come in at the right angle was tricky, because presumably the camera is where Ford's head ought to be.

Shot 37 The picture on the Oklarado license is based on Ed "Big Daddy" Roth. Note the anticipation before the license goes off screen. Ford doesn't move at all in this shot—it actually turned out to be funnier than when he fidgeted. His entire performance relies on facial animation and Torbin's reading.

Shot 38 This scene was originally filled with uncomfortable pauses as the old man stared at Ford. It was funny, but took up too much time, so we tightened it. The pause before the old man says, "whatever" probably should have stayed. The quick cut from this shot to the next was initially intended to cover up the stiffness of the old man's move, but it made an effective edit.

Shot 39 The copy of Rod Queens is suddenly much higher on the shelf. Amazing! Originally, there was a shot of Ford pointing to it, but it wasn't necessary because the cut to this close-up explained it.

Shots 40-44 These were all done as one scene in Flash. The old man's entire line of dialogue was animated as though shot in a continuous take, and then the wallet inserts were placed in layers on top. That way, the wallet shots could be cut in at the right moment, and stay on long enough to make it clear that Ford only has ten bucks. When the editing was finalized, the extra keyframes of the old man under the wallet shots were removed. The wallet is two pieces with the same center point (as opposed to masking the ten dollar bill). The right hand is cut out at the wrist, and the thumb is another piece on top, and those two pieces have the same center points. That way the ten dollar bill could be animated freely between the wallet, fingers and thumb. Originally there was a camera move onto the ten dollar bill close-up, but it distracted from the important point, which is that it's a ten dollar bill.

Shot 45 The bit of fence and road in the background of this shot is actually the same thing seen out the window in shot 37. Ford walks up to his car but we cut away before he has to do something besides a walk cycle. Editing brilliance or animation laziness? You decide.

Shot 46 Getting the elbow right was tricky. The upper arm required considerable squash and stretch to keep the elbow on the door. The hand is actually part of the steering wheel. Although only part of the steering wheel was drawn, the center point is where it would be if it were a complete wheel. That way, it rotates correctly when Ford turns the wheel.

Shot 47 The brown car by the AfterMarket sign is the only "civilian" car in the entire show. But we felt we had to make sure this didn't seem like some fantasyland where every car's a hot rod. The Tudor actually moves on a slight curve in this shot. Moving in a straight line seemed too stiff.

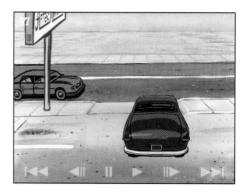

Shot 48 Ford's head tips down in the middle of its turn from left to right, which makes the move more natural. The pivot point for the heads are at the bottom of the ear. There's quite a bit of body language in this one action. Ford really leans to the left. It has to be very clear that Ford has checked that no cars are coming.

Shot 49 This is the same road background first seen in shot 5, except there's no brightness adjustment. The sidewalk is a masked and skewed portion from the background in shot 47. The fence is from shot 45. The brown car and AfterMarket sign help tie this shot back to shot 47 and the next one.

Shot 50 This is an enlarged version of shot 47, but the brown car and AfterMarket sign have been moved in. Ford's car does some overshoot as it screeches to a halt. The brake lights help sell it.

Shot 51 This is a completely still drawing of Ford. It's onscreen for so few frames that the image barely registers as is.

Shot 52 Slow motion is difficult to sell in Flash. Usually it just looks like things moving slowly as opposed to motion that is shown at a slower speed. The guitar plus the contrast between the earlier shot of the Gremlin zipping by help.

Shot 53 Angel whizzes off into the distance on a background that you won't see again. She needed to disappear quickly, so the distance she covers is kind of unrealistic. But then again, her Gremlin is really fast. As it turns out, this whole sequence was swiped from *Enemy of the State*, when Will Smith's character sees Gene Hackman from the back of the cab.

Shot 54 We added Ford's reaction to seeing Angel because cutting to the exterior of Jickett's was too abrupt. We needed to see that Angel had affected Ford.

Shot 55 An establishing shot. Note the way the front end of the Tudor dips down as the car stops. The little stuff counts.

Shot 56 Ford's facial animation was done first, and then the Ford animated symbol was moved on a motion path.

Shot 57 We knew that the hi-jinx that would follow meant that the shop needed to be relatively empty, so we put the car up on the lift. But Mooney is so short, he couldn't possibly work on the car while it's up on the lift, so Doug came up with the image of Jicketts holding Mooney up. Mooney does a lot of squashing and stretching in this shot. The torch cable is done with a line, shape tweens, and lots of keyframing. Jicketts has several replace-ment arms because his hands are in so many different positions. The tummy line that the right hand goes behind is just a line and a shirt-colored chunk to cover up the hand. The image of Jicketts leaning on Mooney was not storyboarded, but came out later in the animation. It's a good example of their relationship.

Shot 58 Another simple Ford reaction shot. There are two Ford torsos, and this one has more of a slouch.

Shot 59 This Jicketts arm-fold was originally in shot 57 when Jicketts leans on Mooney. Originally, Mooney did a lot of sputtering before Jicketts burst out laughing, but we pulled that back because Mooney would have to wait for Jicketts to laugh before he could. Jicketts' laugh is a good example of multi-piece squash and stretch. The head stays the same size but rotates while the arms and body squash and stretch together.

Shot 60 Ford's reaction. Bummer!

Shot 61 The tummy rub wouldn't work if the right arm did not bend at the elbow. Mooney does some pretty extreme squash and stretch in this shot. Jicketts does quite a bit of overshoot when he points to the phone.

Shot 62 Although this shot looks the same as the previous angles, this one is framed slightly differently to point out the phone. This pointing hand was originally going to be used when Ford points to the Rod Queens magazine. Each frame of the torch cable was keyframed individually.

Shot 63 There was originally a lot of ominous dialogue here, but it got pared down to the rapid-fire "Pizza Stop" business.

Shot 64 This third "Pizza Stop" was added after the animatic was done. Funny comes in threes.

Shot 65 More Jicketts squash and stretch. Each arm up and down position is slightly different. Jicketts puts his arms down and then shakes his head. One action at a time.

Shot 66 The Mooney jump uses two different bodies and a lot of arm swinging. Once you have the drawings of the key poses, it's then a matter of getting the tweening right to sell the action.

Show 67 Mooney's hand is cut off at the wrist so that he can actually push the buttons, and then point up as he falls. Otherwise, this is the same body used in the previous shot.

Shot 68 Jicketts has a big round body and tiny legs, so most of his pose and actions come from his arms and head, particularly since he's not a big fan of walking.

Shot 69 After he's done talking, Mooney doesn't move much because he's got some thinking to do. The swaying of the phone cord keeps the shot alive.

Shot 70 This background is actually just a few lines, and various parts of painted backgrounds are masked in. The phone cord should probably sway, but it took too much effort. You may be wondering where the garage door is. Apparently, Jickett's never closes.

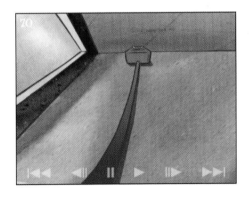

Shot 71 Mooney's so compact it's hard to get a strong silhouette out of him. Here the action is made clear by presenting the phone, then the torch, then the phone on the torch led by the eyes.

Shot 72 The phone's pivot point is right where it rests on the torch. The cable is a simple shape tween.

Shot 73 This shot was originally storyboarded showing Mooney's back, but it was funnier to show his face and tongue as he concentrates. The key to posing Mooney here was to balance his body with the left arm.

Shot 74 This shot works the same way as shot 72, but from a different angle. We needed to clearly show the action, but also misdirect a bit.

Shot 75 This is closer than shot 73 to focus on Mooney's face. You can't exaggerate enough. Notice the anticipatory down squash, then the stretched frame, then the head settles into position. How Mooney manages to get the phone and the torch mixed up when he is clearly holding the torch here will always be an unsolved mystery.

Shot 76 This shot is staged to avoid showing what Mooney has in his hand. The dialogue is not especially important, but it does give Jicketts a chance to launch into more bad beat poetry.

Shot 77 Mooney has to test the sparker first to set up the gag. The hand is in two pieces. One half of the sparker is with the thumb and wrist; the other half is with the palm and fingers. The pivot point is the sparker's pivot coil. The wrist covers up the palm without the need for a mask layer. We tried having Mooney look at Jicketts while he sparks the phone, but it was actually funnier to have him look right at the phone and still try to light it.

Shot 78 Another simple action. The hand is cut out and the wrist piece tapers off to accommodate the hand lines. It was important to show the hand turning the knob, as opposed to using one piece and rotating the entire arm. Another important detail is that he picks his hand up off the knob in between turns.

Shot 79 This shot is all about the sound effect.

Shot 80 This is the second spark attempt. Perhaps a third would have been funnier, but we wanted to keep moving. The next action poses a layout problem because Mooney throws the sparker over his shoulder facing the direction of the garage door (the right side). But the phone is also near the garage door on the left. That Mooney's got great aim.

Shot 81 In this shot, the sparker's center point is dead center, and it simply tweens from right to left rotating counter-clockwise once.

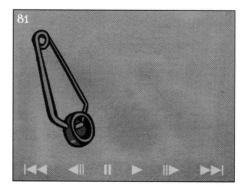

Shot 82 The torch lights, and a frame later the phone bursts into flames. The key to selling the action here was to have the torch rock a bit after it ignites.

Shot 83 We employed a replacement nose for Ford's sniffing action. Smells travel fast at Jickett's Speed Shop.

Shot 84 The flying chunks use the offset centerpoint arc technique. The fire is made up of three replacement shapes colored with a radial gradient with partial transparency in a movie clip.

Shot 85 Staging this shot was difficult because previously it appeared that the Tudor was parked well behind the garage door to Jickett's, so the plastic glob would have to travel around the door to hit the car. But it works because there's no real perspective. Also, it was tough to make the blob stand out against the background, which has several different colors.

Shot 86 The important part of this shot is the shadow, because it indicates just how small this blob is. The guitar riff is the same one from the title card.

Shot 87 Another wild Ford reaction shot where he doesn't move. There's many quick cuts in the following sequence to keep the mayhem level up without having to animate too much per shot. The music is from the Jickett's theme.

Shot 88 We cut to the phone to show what's bothering Jicketts.

Shot 89 Even turban jewels squash and stretch.

Shot 90 Now we see what's bothering Mooney. Note that on the zoom in, the camera overshoots for a more natural move.

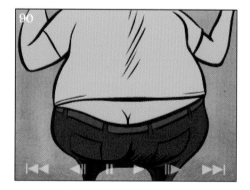

Shot 91 Mooney does the Tex Avery eyes. It wasn't necessary to move the tongue because the focus is on the goofy eye action, but the body does some anticipation.

Shot 92 This shot doesn't make much sense because the car has somehow re-parked itself at a different angle. But we did this because we didn't want to have to show what was happening inside the shop, and because we wanted to make it plausible that Ford might not see Angel drive up. We hope the cut happens fast enough that no one notices.

Shot 93 This is a four-frame walk cycle. The weight is implied by the movement of the fire extinguisher.

Shot 94 The hand is cut off at the wrist to go in front of the car, while the wrist and arm are a separate piece behind the car.

Shot 95 Mooney and the extinguisher hose are one piece that can pivot on top of the extinguisher to really emphasize the power of the spray. The foam is a single chunk scaled and skewed differently in each frame.

Shot 96 The foam hits Jicketts in one frame. Fast is funny. The rest is reaction. He leans back at the hips, flails his arms, and goes back to upright.

Shot 97 This angle of the Gremlin was first seen in shot 28. We used the watercolor blob for the background because we didn't want to make another specialty angle of Jickett's. The body dips when the car stops. The body is cut into two pieces so the tire can fit between them. The piece that goes behind the tire has the wheel well drawn in. Both have the same center point and were moved together.

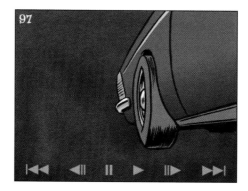

Shot 98 Mooney bounces across the screen this time so the gag keeps building.

Shot 99 This is the same angle of the car from shot 97 with a door chunk and interior placed on top. The boots are the same, but the one on the right has a brightness of −10. The little bit of ankle pivot helps give the step weight, and of course the car rises and settles when Angel steps out of the car completely.

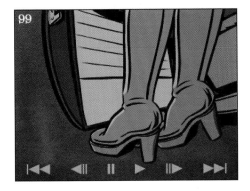

Shot 100 This walk cycle is a cheat, but you never see the legs below the knees so it doesn't matter. The pizza box stays level because the arm is moving it up and down as the body rises and falls.

Shot 101 Mooney shoot across the screen a third time, this time holding on for dear life. Mooney doesn't move at all. Since he's flying across the screen, it wouldn't be noticeable anyway, and would just take up processor power.

Shot 102 Jicketts does a flailing walk, and this is the most movement we've seen from him so far. It's important to keep one foot firmly planted on the ground before the other moves to give the illusion of weight to a fat character.

Shot 103 There's a little bit of overlap on Angel's hair as she turns her head. The hat is one piece, the hair is another, the face and other side of the hair is yet another. Check out the cheat as she drops the pizza box.

Shot 104 The two forearms are the same in this shot. It was difficult to make the pizza look floppy, so we cut away quickly.

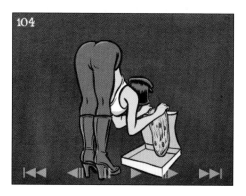

Shot 105 This shot was also a tough one. Angel doesn't have very realistically proportioned anatomy, so different angles of her are hard to draw. Again, cutting quickly helps cover these things up so the movement is what reads. Note the same forearms as in the previous shot.

Shot 106 The squash and stretch, sliding pepperoni, and shadow help make this action work. The sound effect ties it all together.

Shot 107 The extinguisher foam is flipped horizontally and vertically every other frame to keep it moving.

Shot 108 Mooney flies on an arc. The floor is actually the watercolor blob again and some black lines with alpha transparency. Note the setup of the creeper.

Shot 109 It took a lot of tries to get Jicketts to wipe off his face right. The action wasn't fast enough, or the arm was at the wrong angle. Eventually it was a combination of fewer frames, and additional head tilt. The foam is wiped away using an animated mask. A little squash and stretch helps Jicketts' surprise.

Shot 110 This is the only time we see a side view of Jicketts' body. Strictly speaking, he's pointing at the back corner of the shop, but we didn't want to have to account for Ford at this point.

Shot 111 The toilet is cut into front and back pieces instead of using a mask on Mooney's head. This is easier to animate because masks only work when the layers are locked. Mooney must blink once his head is out of the toilet.

Shot 112 Angel, like Ford, doesn't move a whole lot when she talks. She's a very calm person, but we also want a little calm before the Mooney hijinx start up again.

Shots 113-115 This Mooney run is only two frames. The insert is just to clarify that Mooney's stepped on a board with wheels for those unfamiliar with creepers. Note that it pitches up when he steps on it instead of just taking off. This helps emphasize the

wheels. Then Mooney flies across the screen, frozen in place on the creeper.

Shot 116 Angel has the good sense to step out of the way. She should walk towards her car (which isn't pictured in the background), but it took too much effort to make her turn around. Jicketts does some really extreme squash and stretch here.

Shot 117 This toilet-cam seemed like a funny idea and helped isolate the action. If we'd chosen an external angle, the figures would have had to be very small in the frame, and you want to see Jicketts' reaction. Jicketts' hands wave, but a small secondary actions like that are sometimes hard to see when the character is moving quickly.

Shot 118 By going to black we avoid having to animate water, which would basically be cel animation. Also, the action takes place in the viewer's mind, where we hope it becomes more disgusting than it would have been had we animated it.

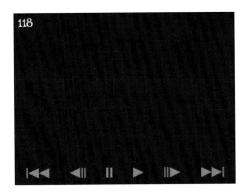

Shot 119 Sometimes the background distorts when Jicketts pumps his fist in the air, which is another potential hazard when using bitmap backgrounds. Jicketts only has two mouth positions here. Mooney has one, and a single arm used at many different rotations. Mooney actually gets off pretty easy here.

Shot 120 Ford sighs here to show that all is well, and he can start paying attention to what's going on around him again. This is the same body used in every shot of this angle. Only the head and hands change.

Shot 121 The Gremlin conveniently covers up Angel's legs to hide the fake walk cycle. The original staging had Angel parking her car in the other direction, but then we would have had to have shown Ford turning his car around, and we wanted to get them together as soon as possible.

Shot 122 This shot didn't work until there was some secondary animation on the hair. Since we weren't going to show Ford actually standing up, it was important to exaggerate his anticipation instead. The rest is implied. We could have shown Ford getting into his car, fumbling with the keys, watching Angel drive off, and finally catching up to her, but it was better just to cut to the next shot.

Shot 123 Finally, Ford and Angel are together, which we've been waiting for since he first saw her. This is another trick angle because the Tudor doesn't quite match the perspective of the Gremlin. But this framing makes it believable. Ford is part of the car symbol up until it finishes its overshoot. Then the symbol is broken apart and the pieces (also symbols) are spread out onto layers within the main timeline. Ford can be animated easily this way.

Shot 124 There's quite a bit of cutting during dialogue in this sequence. Doing this gives your editing a little more sophistication than cutting at the end (or beginning) of a line, but it means that your shots have to be combined into a single timeline. Ford's head is animated doing the entire line, and the same symbol is used in the two-shot and the closer shot.

Shot 125 Again, Angel started her line in the previous shot, and continues it here. Angel was animated entirely within the Gremlin, and then the Gremlin symbol was animated leaving the frame.

Shot 126 This shot is a deliberate callback to shot 54 when Angel first left him in the dust. The background is the same one first seen in shot 5.

Shot 127 Torben actually stood across the room and shouted this dialogue at the microphone. To get the proper illusion of driving side-by-side, the two cars not only move back and forth, but also up and down slightly.

Shot 128 The sign that whizzes by is really the only visual indicator of speed, so the sound effects are really critical here.

Shot 129 This is another quick cut to hide slight perspective problems. It wasn't necessary to make Ford's head turn to follow the Gremlin because it would hardly be noticeable. Although the background painting is completely static, the divider lines and the signs tend to cover this up. Besides, the focus should be on the main action of the cars.

Shot 130 This shot sets up the second to last shot of the show so the audience is familiar with the shot angle. The dashboard, roof, doors and windshield are all one piece. The seat backs are another, and Ford is sandwiched in between. It also shows the action in a way that Flash can handle fairly easily. Otherwise, we either would have had to resort to the overhead shot again, or draw lots more car angles. Unacceptable!

Shot 131 To make this perspective work, the Tudor actually starts at the vanishing point well off the road, but it matches as it comes into frame. So far this is the only stoplight in *Jicketts*. The glowing lights were done the same way the headlights were: single color radial gradients going from solid to 0% alpha.

Shot 132 That Ford never gives up, even when a girl tries to run him off the road. Dogged persistence is one of his character traits, and having him jump through these hoops was a way to show that without resorting to exposition.

Shot 133 Angel blinks at the exact moment she decides to race him, and it lasts for three frames. She lures him in slowly. In earlier drafts, she made light of his name and the car's manufacturer being the same, but it took too long and it made her a little too condescending to him.

Shot 134 This shot is zoomed back slightly from shot 132. The idea is that Ford would get smaller and Angel would get bigger in frame, to show her dominating him. Ford's reaction when Angel cuts him off is pretty funny, but no one seems to laugh when they see it, perhaps because it's not exaggerated enough.

Shot 135 Angel is larger in frame here than in shot 133. She probably should have moved a bit to emphasize, "would it?" but the eyebrows seemed to do the trick. Angel's acting has to be fairly subtle, unlike the other characters. Tess' southern accent slips out a little here. Angel's ethnicity is unspecified and isn't particularly important, but we had in mind that she was Latino, like Jicketts.

Shot 136 The exact moment when she clicks in the lighter was tough to choose. If it happened too early, it got lost during the dialogue exchange. If it happened too late, it would click out unrealistically fast. We had to create suspense without tipping our hand as to what she was going to do with the lighter. Originally, we had a shot of her leaning over as she pushed in the lighter, which Ford takes as a flirtation. We have no problem being sexist pigs, but the shot had to go when the staging of the cars put Angel on the other side of the Tudor.

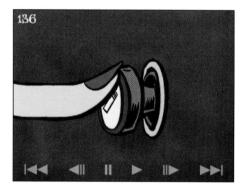

Shot 137 Ford is smaller still. This is a new hand. The fingers that never move, but still give the pose a lot of expression.

Shot 138 Angel nearly fills the screen now. Tess really nailed the shift in attitude.

Shot 139 The lighter is made of four parts: the outer sleeve, the lighter itself and the mask layer (to cover up the portion that would stick out past the sleeve), and the inner sleeve to go behind the lighter. Using just a mask wouldn't have worked because of the varied shape of the lighter. Also, the mask shape sometimes causes a slight halo on monitors not set to millions of colors, which is particularly noticeable on bitmap backgrounds. Don't forget the overshoot, particularly with mechanical objects.

Shot 140 Switching to Ford's point-of-view seemed to be the best way to show this action. Having the glowing end fly right at the camera helped sell the idea that it was hot.

Shot 141 In theory, this shot is a continuity error, because the lighter should come in through the passenger side window. But it was less effective to frame Ford facing the other direction and show the lighter falling in his lap, so we cheated. No one ever notices. Even though Ford's entire arm isn't drawn, it should be treated as though it were. The pivot point should be where the elbow would be so it bends realistically. If not, where the elbow would be should be taken into account in the animation.

Shot 142 This shot is another slight head-scratcher, because the Gremlin ought to be in the other lane. Maybe she changed lanes. Between this and the previous shot there was supposed to be a shot of the signal turning green, but it just slowed things down.

Shot 143 Angel's back in the right lane. D'oh!

Shot 144 Now Ford is suddenly behind Angel. The previous shot would have been the place to show Ford changing lanes, but the car's perspective wouldn't allow it. This shot is a little bait-and-switch because it required too much visual exposition to explain that Angel has tricked Ford into following her to a freeway off-ramp. Instead, it's just a complete surprise. However, we planned to account for this in the following episode.

Shot 145 When blowing something up to fill the screen, it is unnecessary to make the object fill the screen with the last keyframe. Doing that only makes the zoom go too fast. Instead, keyframe the last bit of the object you want to see last, and then go to a rectangle of color, in this case black. Also, if you're zooming multiple objects, such as Ford and the steering wheel, as soon as an object goes out of frame, put in a blank keyframe and get it off the stage. Otherwise, Flash has to do the calculations on an object no one will ever see, and it slows down the animation.

To be continued...

IT'S A WRAP!

So there you have it—a detailed rundown on the making of the first episode of *Jickett's Speed Shop*. It's a good bet that you didn't notice half of the subtle touches when you watched the episode initially. That's why it's essential to study the classics frame-by-frame. If you haven't taken a look at the specially prepared version with DVD-like controls, crack open the CD that comes with this book. You'll see each and every move. The following appendix delivers the skinny on cleaning up your movies, as well as pre-loading, and output to video.

A Pull Up to
the Window

So you've written the coolest story, created the most intriguing characters, and built yourself a wicked cartoon. It's time to get that Flash movie ready for the Internet. This appendix touches on the things you'll want to do before transferring that masterpiece to your web server.

CLEAN-UP

It's more than just file size, Flash fans. You want to make your movies snappy *and* happy. Test your movies carefully, checking for data-heavy frames with Flash's Bandwidth Profiler. If you spot a bandwidth-hogging frame, you should be able to pinpoint why it's so large. Perhaps there's a bitmap image, or a new Movie Clip. If you're not sure, it may be that you've accidentally broken apart a symbol on that frame.

Here are some additional clean-up hints:

- *No mystery tweens*—If you have anything in your Library called Tween 1, Tween 2, Tween 12, etc., it means you have a tween using chunks that aren't symbols. Anything that moves or will appear more than once in your movie should be a symbol. Otherwise you're duplicating data.

- *Use Movie Clips wherever possible to save on size*—Movie Clips must load in entirely, and then they can loop indefinitely without much additional data. Used as animated symbols, however, every time the animated symbol loops, the keyframe data must be loaded again. It's as though you had the keyframes repeating in the main Timeline. For certain things, like walk cycles, using animated symbols can't be avoided; but in other cases where it would not matter if the Timeline stopped and the symbol kept moving, use Movie Clips. (Flash 5 makes new symbols Movie Clips by default.)

- *Optimize symbols, if you must*—You may find that doing so does not substantially decrease the size of your files. If it's a large object that must move quickly on the screen, optimizing is a good idea; otherwise, a little more detail usually leads to a better-looking cartoon.

- *Don't break apart text unless absolutely necessary*—Once broken apart, the text is uneditable. Editable text is bandwidth-friendly because Flash only needs to load each letter that gets used once, and if it's used again it's treated as an instance. So if you use the word "poop", the letters p and o get loaded in, and then you get the other o and p for free.

PRELOADING

Preloading is a necessary evil. If you don't use a preloader, as soon as there's a new chunk in the Timeline that hasn't been loaded, everything stops until that chunk has been loaded. Unintentional pauses are not funny.

Streaming sound takes up the bulk of the bandwidth, so there's even less opportunity for chunks to stream to the viewer. Unfortunately, there's really no way of knowing how much you should preload because there's no way to be sure what kind of connection the user has. Just because they have a 56k modem doesn't mean they're connecting at 56k.

Setting up a preloader is pretty straightforward—you'll likely use an If Frame Is Loaded action to set the specific frame or label. If you want to play it safe, preload the entire thing (or almost the entire thing). This means you don't have to worry about the movie stopping while something loads, but it also means that there's a long wait before anything plays.

Otherwise, you'll just have to pick a base-level connection speed, and preload enough to cover the movie at that speed. You can check this by using the streaming graph when you use Test Movie. Watch the green line, which indicates how much has streamed in, or loaded. The green line should always be ahead of the currently playing frame. If the current frame catches up with the green line, you need to preload more.

Another preloading scheme is to load all your symbols up front and then play the movie while the sound streams in. As long as you give the sound a short head start, this usually works fine. Put every symbol that gets used in the movie in a frame after the If Frame Is Loaded loop but before the frame the movie starts on (the frame that the If Frame Is Loaded action will Go To and Play to). If you have any sounds used as Event sounds, add them in a keyframe with the volume turned off. You'll still want to pre-load some of the streaming sound to cover yourself.

You can fake a progress bar by spreading the symbols out over several frames. Try to evenly divide the data (which you can check when you Test Movie). Suppose you spread them out over five frames. As each frame of symbols loads in, that's another 20% loaded. The progress bar will simply jump a whopping 20% instead of slowly moving in increments, but at least it tells the user that something is happening.

While not essential, it's always nice to provide something for the viewer to do while the movie loads. The first episode of *Jickett's Speed Shop* includes The Kustomizer, which allows folks to chop, channel, section, skirt, flame, and paint Ford's cool ride.

DUMPING FLASH TO VIDEO

Flash can easily be exported to QuickTime; however, be aware that all Movie Clips must first be converted to animated symbols. Turning your Flash bits to QuickTime allows you to bring them into Adobe After Effects for the one-two punch. You can add motion blur, deal with bitmaps easily, use filters—all the things Flash won't do. After Effects is a very powerful animation program, but the chunks still have to come from somewhere, and Flash is as good a place as any thanks to its drawing tools. The Flash Timeline is good for replacement animation, where you swap different chunks in and out. This sort of thing is a real hassle in After Effects, but there's one big important tip you need to know.

The "Falpha" Channel

Suppose you want to take an animated Flash element and export it as a QuickTime with an alpha channel. While Flash appears to support this, there's a hitch. Choose 32-bit Color (alpha channel) as a Format option. When you bring the QuickTime movie into After Effects, it will appear to have no alpha channel. (Or there is, but it's just a slight halo around the object.) Strangely, if you export a single frame, that will give you an alpha channel with no problems. So is exporting a series of frames the only way around this?

Not if you use the "Falpha" Channel technique (the name is either short for "Flash Alpha," or is derived from Harrison Ford's character in *American Graffiti*). All you do is create a new layer above everything else. Make a rectangle that covers the entire Stage. In the color mixer, choose white and then set the alpha to 0%. Fill the rectangle with this transparent color. Now export the animation as a QuickTime, and it'll have a proper alpha channel. Why? Who can say? At least this works.

Let's Go to the Videotape

Getting the QuickTime movies off your computer and onto videotape requires a video output card. At Twinkle we take the high route and use a Media 100. There are a number of vendors that offer less expensive solutions. Check out the cards from ATI, Matrox and others. You'll want to look for a card that provides VGA-to-NTSC conversion, along with audio and video output jacks, in order to hook directly to a VCR.

Why bother with video? It gives you a constant frame rate. Do all the alpha tweening and chunk moving you want; video doesn't blink at that kind of stuff. You won't have to worry about whether or not the person who wants to look at your cartoon has the latest version of the plug-in (you'd be surprised how many people think they have it but don't), or if they're using a laptop with a crummy screen, or if they don't have a sound card. Conditions vary wildly once you step out of the saftey of your own machine, and never with greater certainty than when you're trying to impress someone. Besides, are you really going to force your grandmother to buy a computer and figure out how to use it just so she can watch your brand spankin' new cartoon?

Why not just go out electronically? The advantage of distribution via videotape or DVD allows your cartoon play in venues without a PC or Mac. (Yes, indeed … there are still places without computers.)

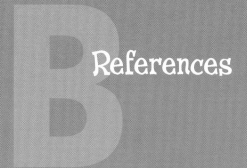

References

While reading through these pages, you'll have come across a number of books that are worthy of recommendation. While we could give you a massive list of additional reading material, it's likely that you won't be able to get them all, anyway. On the following page we give you must haves. If nothing else, get the Preston Blair books.

RECOMMENDED READING

Cartoon Animation by Preston Blair (Walter Foster Publishing). *Cartoon Animation* is an easily available hefty paperback that combines the two original books. If you can, get the two giant-size volumes—*Animation : Learn How to Draw Animated Cartoons* and *How to Animate Film Cartoons*—that make up this book because the oversized format is really much more useful.

Animation : Learn How to Draw Animated Cartoons (How to Draw and Paint Series, No. 26) has been slightly reformatted, with a new cover bearing the title Cartoon Animation, but the original cover and all the illustrations are reproduced inside.

How to Animate Film Cartoons (How to Draw and Paint Series, No. 190)

Disney Animation: The Illusion of Life by Frank Thomas and Ollie Johnston (Abbeville). This one can be hard to find, but there are available copies out there (check eBay). There's even a short-run signed edition, although this version is extremely expensive.

Cartooning the Head and Figure by Jack Hamm (Perigee, June 1982)

The Five C's of Cinematography: Motion Picture Filming Techniques by Joseph V. Mascelli (Silman-James Press, June 1998)

Screenplay: The Foundations of Screenwriting by Syd Field (DTP)

How To Succeed in Animation by Gene Deitch. This one's online for free at http://genedeitch.awn.com.

The Animator's Survival Kit by Richard Williams (Faber & Faber)

WEBSITES

You can turn to the web for a host of information and amusement. Here are some of the (un)usual suspects:

Twinkle Sites

Come visit the core of the Twinkle universe.

Twinkleland! www.twinkleland.com

Jicketts Speed Shop www.jicketts.com

idiotland.com www.idiotland.com
Your Source for Freeform Stupidity!

More Sites by John Kuramoto

John's built a lot of sites over the years. Here are some of his favorites.

Doug Allen's site www.dougallencomics.com

Ghost World www.ghostworld-themovie.com

Richard Sala's site www.richardsala.com

Jimmy Corrigan click-o-rama www.randomhouse.com/knopf/pantheon/graphicnovels/acme.html

The David Boring "trailer" www.randomhouse.com/knopf/pantheon/graphicnovels/flash.html

Other Fave Sites

Here are some more sites we dig. We hope you dig them, too.

Fantagraphics www.fantagraphics.com
Looking for something jolly to read? How about Idiotland, or perhaps some Steven?

Jim Woodring's site www.jimwoodring.com

Mark Newgarden's site www.laffpix.com

The personal website of Rodney Alan Greenblat,
and the Center For Advanced Whimsy www.whimsyload.com

Lane Smith and Jon Scieszka's website www.chucklebait.com

J. Otto Seibold's site www.jotto.com

The Ragtime Ephemeralist site www.wwa.com/~weese/
The closest you'll get to a Chris Ware homepage.

WFMU www.wfmu.org
Freeform radio at its finest. Wednesday night from 6 to 7pm
eastern is Seven Second Delay time, but you can dig into the
archives whenever you like.

JOHN K'S TOP 12 FAVORITE FUNNY MOVIES

So John, tell us your top twelve funny movies …

The Producers Mel Brooks

This is Spinal Tap Rob Reiner

Raising Arizona The Coen Brothers

Some Like it Hot Billy Wilder

Dr. Strangelove Stanley Kubrick

The Graduate Mike Nichols

The Chaplin Mutuals Charlie Chaplin (but if I had to pick one,
"One A.M." the one with the wall bed)

Sherlock Jr. Buster Keaton (there's plenty of great Buster Keaton
films, but this one makes me laugh the most)

The Dark Backward Adam Rifkin

Sleeper Woody Allen

Battlefield Earth Roger Christian (but it's Travolta's fault)

JOHN K'S TOP 12 "BATTERY RECHARGERS"

These aren't necessarily my favorite films (although some are),
but they're the ones I watch when creativity wanes.

2001 Stanley Kubrick (could be my all-time favorite film)

The City of Lost Children Jeunet & Caro

The Adventures of Baron Munchausen Terry Gilliam

Touch of Evil Orson Welles

Blade Runner Ridley Scott

North by Northwest Alfred Hitchcock

The Killer John Woo (It's often a toss-up between *The Killer*
and *Hard Boiled*)

Raging Bull Martin Scorsese

Fight Club David Fincher

Dark City Alex Proyas

My Neighbor Totoro Hayao Miyazaki

Toy Story 2 John Lasseter, Ash Brannon, Lee Unkrich

And once in a while, *Showgirls*.

Building a
Better Button

Ready to banish those boring buttons? This appendix will help you to create works of button genius—clickable masterpieces that set your projects apart from the crowd.

EASY-CLICK TEXT BUTTONS

Nothing is worse than a text button that only works when the mouse is over a portion of a letter. When you make a text button, you should always create a hit area for it. This is one extra step that makes everyone's lives easier, so in the name of human decency, follow these steps:

1. Set a keyframe in the Hit frame so it contains a copy of the text as shown in Figure C.1.
2. Using the Rectangle tool, draw a box slightly larger than the text (Figure C.2). A stroke does not affect the hit area.
3. Delete the text in the Hit frame, if you want. Group the rectangle and the button label, as shown in Figure C.3.

   If you're feeling extra miserly about file size you can use a rectangle symbol as the hit area, although a rectangle takes up less than 1k.

Figure C.2 The rectangle will make the button easier to click.

Figure C.1 The (duplicate) text in place.

Figure C.3 That's it!

BUTTONS AS ENTERTAINMENT

Buttons can be highly entertaining things all by themselves. Suppose you take the little robot from Chapter 3 (see Figure C.4), and you want her to jump when you click her. So you make a button. Put the robot in the Up frame; then put a movie clip of the jumping robot in the Down frame. And you make a rectangle covering the robot in the Hit frame. Right?

Figure C.4
Remember me?

Well, the problem with that is the robot only jumps as long as the mouse button is held down. As soon as you let go of the mouse button, the robot snaps back to the Up pose. If you click fast, you barely see it at all. Unacceptable!

The way to fix it is to not make it a button. Instead, you make a dummy hit area that drives a movie clip of the robot. The movie clip is stopped on the first frame, and is the equivalent of the Up frame. The rest of the movie clip is the jumping action;

when it's done, it goes back to the first frame and stops. When you click the dummy hit area, it tells the movie clip to play the jumping action, which plays all the way through whether the mouse is over the hit area or not.

The Jumping Robot Button

While you can use the file you created in Chapter 3 for the pieces in this exercise, you'll probably want to open **buttons.fla** from the Appendix C folder on the CD-ROM, instead. (The **buttons.fla** file will have all of the symbols loaded in its Library.) Once you have the goods loaded, follow these steps to build a simple jumping robot button:

1. In the movie clip of the robot jumping, add a layer for actions, and put a Stop action on the first frame, as shown in Figure C.5.

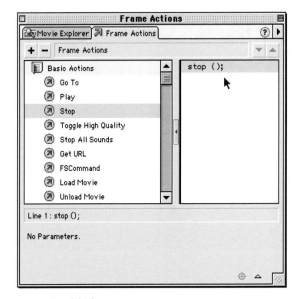

Figure C.5 Stop right there.

2. Drag the robot movie clip onto the Stage. In the Instance palette, make sure the Behavior is Movie Clip, and give this instance a name (see Figure C.6). This is so that the dummy hit area knows which movie clip to affect.

Figure C.6 A name is required for the dummy hit area to know which movie clip to affect.

3. Draw a rectangle slightly larger than the robot. This is your hit area. Group the rectangle and make it a button, as shown in Figure C.7.

4. Edit the hit area button. Move the keyframe with the rectangle over to the Hit frame (see Figure C.8).

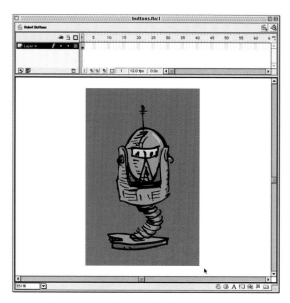

Figure C.7 The rectangle provides a nice big hit area.

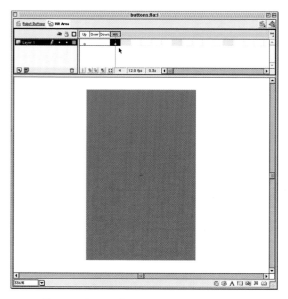

Figure C.8 The rectangle, moved.

5. The hit area button on the stage should now be a translucent blue as shown in Figure C.9. This is what Flash does to a button that has nothing in the Up position.

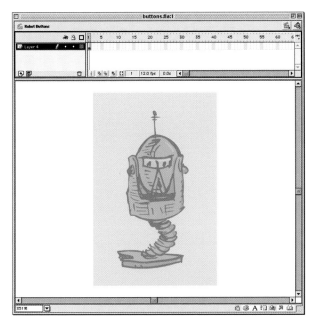

Figure C.9 You can see the hit area, but it won't show up when you export.

6. Select the hit area. Add a Tell Target with the Object Actions window (see Figure C.10).

7. Click in the Target text box at the bottom. Either type in the name of your robot movie clip, or click the Insert Target Path button (the little target-shaped button down at the bottom to open a new window. Click the name of your robot movie clip (Figure C.11) and then click OK.

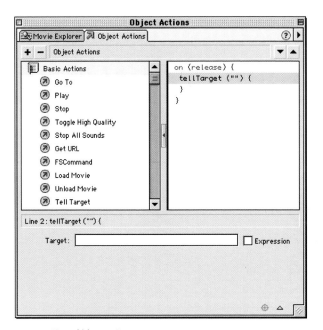

Figure C.10 Now which target?

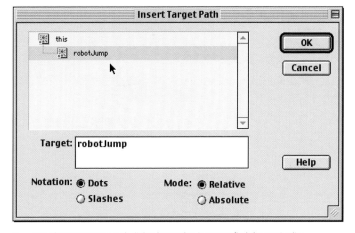

Figure C.11 The Insert Target Path dialog box makes it easy to find the movie clip.

8. Add a Go To with the Object Actions window, and change the frame number to 2, as shown in Figure C.12.

Figure C.12 That's all there is to it.

Test the movie and see how much jollier the button is now. If you want the jump to happen as soon as the button gets pressed, go back into the Object Actions window and change the "on (release)" to "on (press)" instead (Figure C.13).

So, why not just use a play action in step 8? You can, and it'll work, but when you press the button, it plays the current frame and then the rest, so there's a pause of 1/12 of a second (if the frame rate is 12fps) before the jump starts. Fast is funny.

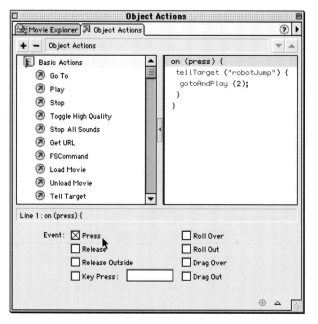

Figure C.13 Now the robot will jump when the button is pressed, rather than when the button is released.

> **TIP** Looking for a shortcut? Use Robot Button Movie with Over action from the Library in **buttons.fla**. You can simply swap symbols (with the first robot symbol) and skip steps 1 through 5. And even if you don't swap symbols, you may still want to go into this symbol and poke around.

The Two-Stage Robot Button

What if you want the robot to do something when you mouse over her and then jump when you click? Here's the recipe:

1. In the timeline of the robot movie clip, add some frames past the end of the jump animation. Create a little looping animation for the robot to perform on mouseover, as shown in Figure C.14.

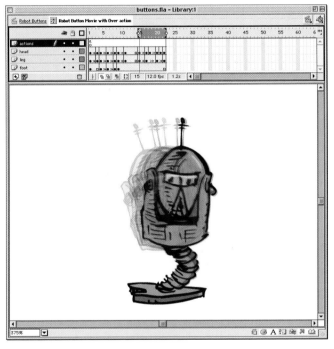

Figure C.14 Add a little sproing.

2. In the Actions layer, add a keyframe 1 frame after the end of the jump animation (frame 12). Add a Go To and Stop action. The default is to stop on frame 1, which is what you want in this case (Figure C.15).

3. In the Actions layer, add a keyframe at the start of the mouseover animation. Label it "over," as shown in Figure C.16.

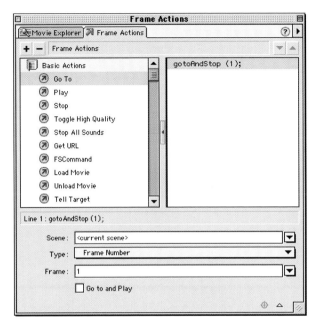

Figure C.15 Go To and Stop on frame 1.

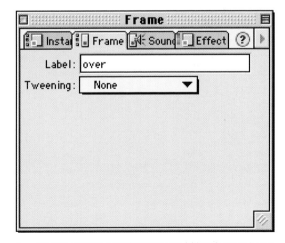

Figure C.16 You can name it anything you want (although "over" is easy to remember).

4. If the last keyframes of your mouseover looping animation are the same as the first, add a keyframe in the Actions layer on the same frame as the last keyframes. If the last keyframes of the looping animation are different than the first, add a keyframe in the Actions layer after the last keyframes, as shown in Figure C.17.

Figure C.17 Keyframes added.

5. Add a Go To and Play action at this keyframe, and make it go to the frame labeled "over" (Figure C.18).

6. Go back to the main timeline. Click on the hit area. Add a Tell Target action. Change the On Event to Roll Over (make sure to uncheck Release). Put in the target name (the robot's instance name). You may want to change the instance name to differentiate it from the previous jumping button example, as shown in Figure C.19.

Figure C.18 Go To and Play "over."

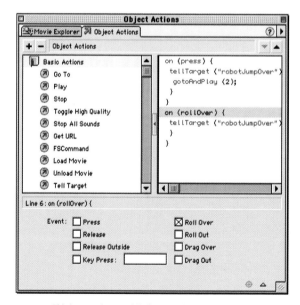

Figure C.19 This instance is named "robotJumpOver."

7. Add a Go To and Play action to the Tell Target. The type is Frame label, and the frame is over (Figure C.20).

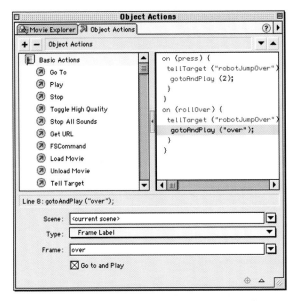

Figure C.20 When the mouse is over the hit area, the robot starts playing the Over animation.

8. In the Object Actions window, click the last curly bracket (}) and add another Tell Target action. Add the target name, and change the On Event to Roll Out. (See Figure C.21.)

9. Add a Go To And Stop action. You want it to stop on frame 1 when the mouse rolls out of the hit area, as shown in Figure C.22.

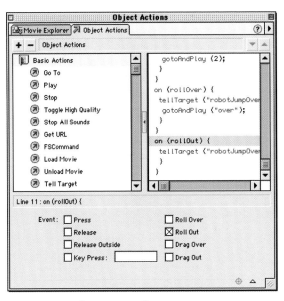

Figure C.21 We got roll over, we got roll out.

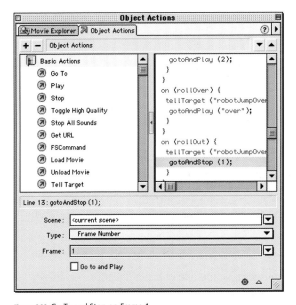

Figure C.22 Go To and Stop on Frame 1.

There is a fatal flaw to this technique—the robot jumps when you click, but if you mouse off the hit area during the jump, the robot will snap back to frame 1. Also, the robot waves her head when you mouse over, but when you mouse off, again she snaps back to frame 1. This looks fine sometimes, but crappy other times. If these things really drive you crazy, there's a way around that, but it requires even more ActionScripting.

It's a dilemma of logic. When you mouse over, the robot movie clip goes to and plays the over animation. When you click, it goes to and plays the jump animation. But there's a command telling the button that when you mouse off, to go to and stop on the first frame. The button will follow that command whether or not it disrupts the animation, because Flash doesn't care. It's only following orders.

This wasn't a problem when the robot only needed to jump when clicked. That's because there was no need for a command on mouse over and a command on mouse out. But now that there is, the solution is to make Flash ask questions. The looping animation should finish the animation and then ask, "Is the mouse still on the hit area? If so, I'll keep looping. If not, I'll go to and stop on the first frame."

1. In the hit area's actions, remove the On Roll Out actions. Choose Actions. Set Variable. Call the variable something descriptive, such as "rollOut" (because this is the thing that tells Flash whether you've rolled out or not). Type in **true** in the value field (or click on it in Functions) and make sure you check the Expression box, as shown in Figure C.23. This makes the value true (as opposed to the letters t, r, u, and e).

2. Under the Roll Over action, add Set Variable again. The variable is the same as the one you set in step 1, but this time the value is **false** (Figure C.24). You can also copy and paste the Set Variable command from step 1.

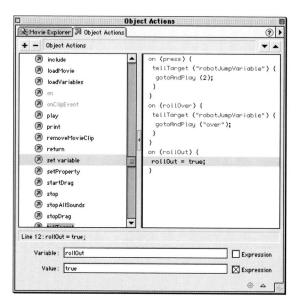

Figure C.23 Setting the True variable.

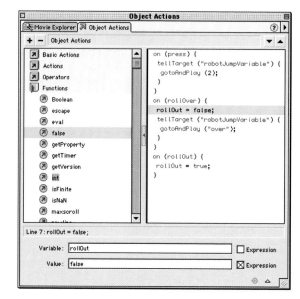

Figure C.24 Setting the False variable.

3. Edit the robot movie clip with the mouseover animation loop. In the action keyframe at the end that's currently set to go to and play over, add an If command from the Actions. Move the go to and play command under the if command. In the if command Condition, type Number(../:rollOut) == Number(false) but change "rollOut" to whatever you picked for a variable name (Figure C.25).

Test the movie and enjoy the new and improved robot jumping jolliness. This ActionScript formula works as long as the mouse over looping animation is the last thing in the movie clip timeline. If it isn't, add an else statement to the if loop (see Figure C.26), or simply add another action keyframe after the if command and make that a Go To and Stop action.

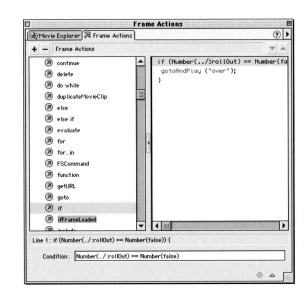

Figure C.25 Setting the Condition.

Say What?

If you really must know what that whole if command business was about, here's the deal. Number means "convert the thing in parentheses to a numerical value that Flash can understand." To computers, false is 0 and true is 1, but to humans, true and false mean more, so we use that for clarity. The gobbledygook means "change to a numerical value the variable called 'rollOut' in the parent timeline." The double equals signs mean equals. "Number(false)" to Flash means 0. So it's an extremely roundabout way of asking if rollOut is false.

Figure C.26 Add that or else!

INDEX

Note to the reader: Throughout this index **boldfaced** page numbers indicate primary discussions of a topic. *Italicized* page numbers indicate illustrations.

Photoshop 6

Hands-on Learning Without All the Classroom Expense!

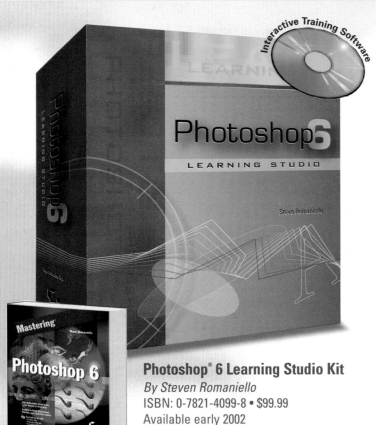

Interactive Training Software

Photoshop® 6 Learning Studio Kit
By Steven Romaniello
ISBN: 0-7821-4099-8 • $99.99
Available early 2002

Mastering™ Photoshop 6
book included free!
(a $39.99 value)

Nothing beats the hands-on training of the **Photoshop 6 Learning Studio**™ when learning complex graphics applications. It's above and beyond the video instruction you'd receive from other "training software." An Adobe-certified trainer steps you through narrated interactive lessons taught at your own pace using proven projects and techniques created so you learn—not watch. Then you can practice your skills using the simulated Photoshop interface.

- Interactive, step-by-step, hands-on lessons offer a level of learning not offered by any other software training product

- Contains 2 semesters of instructional material and 16 hours of dynamic interactive instruction and projects

- Comprehensive coverage of all features you need to become a Photoshop expert

- Simulated interface offers real-world training without the need to buy Photoshop

- Use the Photoshop 6 Learning Studio as a tool for acquiring valuable skills, and then as a fully-searchable reference for quick answers after you have mastered the basics

Coming Soon: Check www.sybex.com for a free demo!

SYBEX®

TELL US WHAT YOU THINK!

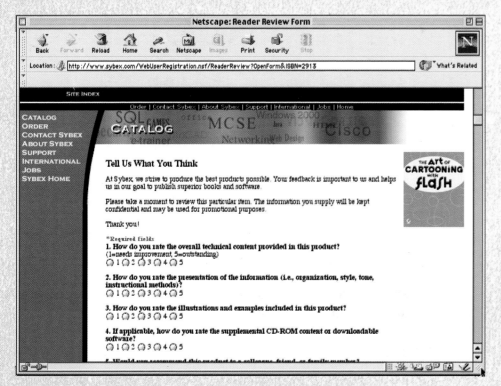

Your feedback is critical to our efforts to provide you with the best books and software on the market. Tell us what you think about the products you've purchased. It's simple:

1. Visit the Sybex website
2. Go to the product page
3. Click on **Submit a Review**
4. Fill out the questionnaire and comments
5. Click **Submit**

With your feedback, we can continue to publish the highest quality computer books and software products that today's busy graphics and Web professionals deserve.

www.sybex.com

SYBEX Inc. • 1151 Marina Village Parkway, Alameda, CA 94501 • 510-523-8233

WHAT'S ON THE CD

The CD is packed full of .FLA exercise files (more on that in a moment) and cool .SWF Flash movie files. It also contains demo versions of important software. So if you don't currently own a copy of Flash, you can install the demo version and start working right away.

The demo software includes:

- Adobe Photoshop (30-day trial for Mac and PC)
- Bias Peak VST (30-day trial)
- Bias Peak LE (limited 30-day trial)
- Bias Deck (30-day trial)
- Macromedia Flash (30-day trial for Mac and PC)
- Sonic Foundry Sound Forge (demo for PC)

TIP If you're a student, you should never pay the retail price for an expensive piece of software (like Flash). Instead, you should investigate the educational versions, which provide full functionality at a greatly reduced price. Save your money for pizza, dude!

You'll also find a whole bunch of jolly Twinkle-created Flash movies on the CD. The Twinkle Vault contains some of Twinkle's earliest work, warts and all. There's the very first Twinkle animation (the Beef Baron Load Screen), a bunch of buttons, and the "silent" version of Shopping Spree!

There's Twinkle Trinkets, Flash chunks to satisfy all your "interactive" needs. Check out the Idiotwriter and the Instant Content Generator for ideas for cartoons.

The Twinkle Animation folder has the "talkie" version of Shopping Spree!, several previously unseen animations, and Quicktimes made using the 1-2 punch of Flash and After Effects.

The Jickett's Speed Shop folder has the pilot episode (with better sound and bitmap quality than the online version), the Jickett's Controller, which allows you to scrutinize every frame, a Quicktime of the Animatic, and the script in Acrobat PDF format.

In the Richard Sala folder, there are two cartoons from www.richardsala.com: The Chuckling Whatsit, based on his graphic novel of the same name, and Peculia, from his comic book series *Evil Eye*, both published by Fantagraphics Books.

The Daniel Clowes folder has the David Boring Trailer, created to coincide with the publication of Clowes' graphic novel *David Boring* by Pantheon, with music by The Irreversible Slacks!

And finally, in the Chris Ware folder is the Jimmy Corrigan "non-animation" based on the dustjacket of his monumental *Jimmy Corrigan* graphic novel, also published by Pantheon.